THE
INSPIRED
VEGETARIAN

THE
INSPIRED
VEGETARIAN

CREATIVE IDEAS FOR
NATURAL, HEALTHY EATING

Christine Ingram

HERMES
HOUSE

This edition produced in 2001 by Hermes House

©Anness Publishing Ltd 2001

This edition published by Hermes House
an imprint of
Anness Publishing Limited
Hermes House
88-89 Blackfriars Road
London SE1 8HA

A CIP catalogue record for this book is available from the British Library

Publisher: Joanna Lorenz
Designers: Patrick McLeavy and Siân Keogh
Photography and styling: Patrick McLeavy and Tom Odulate

Front cover: Lisa Tai, Designer; Thomas Odulate, Photographer;
Helen Trent, Stylist; Marie-Ange Lapierre, Home Economist

Previously published as part of a larger compendium, *The Complete Encyclopedia of Vegetables and Vegetarian Cooking*

Printed and bound in Hong Kong/China

© Anness Publishing Limited 1998, 1999
Updated © 2000
1 3 5 7 9 10 8 6 4 2

NOTES

For all recipes, quantities are given in both metric and imperial measures and, where
appropriate, measures are also given in standard cups and spoons. Follow one set, but not a
mixture, because they are not interchangeable.

Standard spoon and cup measures are level.
I tsp = 5ml, I tbsp = 15ml, I cup = 8 fl oz

Australian standard tablespoons are 20ml. Australian readers should use 3 tsp in place of
I tbsp for measuring small quantities of gelatine, cornflour, salt etc

Medium eggs should be used unless otherwise stated.

CONTENTS

~

INTRODUCTION
6

SOUPS & STARTERS
10

LIGHT MEALS
28

DINNERS
48

SALADS & SIDE DISHES
82

INDEX
96

INTRODUCTION

Committed vegetarians know that a diet excluding meat and fish need not be boring, but perhaps few people realize just how appetizing and attractive vegetarian dishes can be. This book is packed with truly superb recipes for special occasions. Even if your guests are normally committed meat-eaters, they will be delighted by any of these succulent dishes, and friends who are already vegetarians will be amazed by their range and variety.

Vegetables may play the starring role in a recipe or they may be combined with other ingredients, such as rice or pasta. These sorts of dishes are loved for the harmony of their flavour, rather than for the taste of the individual vegetables from which they have been made. However, you will also find many recipes in the following pages that make the most of particular vegetables, so that the specific virtues of each can be appreciated to the full. There is a mix of classic dishes from around the world, such as Gazpacho, Italian Roast Peppers, Hot Sour Chick-peas and Greek Stuffed Vegetables, together with others that have been devised to make the most of individual ingredients. Try, for example, Roast Asparagus Crêpes, Spinach Ravioli, Baked Marrow in Parsley Sauce or Vegetables Julienne with a Red Pepper Coulis.

The book is divided into four chapters: Soups & Starters, Light Meals, Dinners, and Salads & Side Dishes. All the recipes are vegetarian and many are suitable for vegans. They are all very flexible and can easily be adapted to include your own favourite ingredients or vegetables in season. All look tempting and there is something suitable for every occasion when you are entertaining, whether your neighbours are joining you for a weekend brunch, you are giving a formal dinner party or enjoying a special family gathering.

THE VEGETARIAN LARDER

The basis of the vegetarian diet is, of course, formed by vegetables of all kinds. However, many other ingredients are required, both for their individual culinary qualities and for a healthy, balanced diet. There can easily be a shortfall of some essential nutrients, such as iron, in the vegetarian diet and vegans need to be especially scrupulous about including a wide variety of different foods.

FLOURS

Have a selection of different flours to ring the changes. Often it is a good idea to mix two types together in baking for flavour and texture. Use half wholemeal and half plain white flours for a lighter brown pastry crust. Mix buckwheat flour with plain white for crêpes. Flour is a good source of protein, as well as complex starchy carbohydrate. Brown/wholemeal flours do not keep as long as more refined flours.

RICE

The best rice is basmati, an elegant, fragrant, long grain rice, grown in the foothills of the Himalayas. Traditionally eaten with curries, basmati is marvellous in almost all savoury rice dishes. Brown basmati is a lighter wholegrain rice with higher levels of dietary fibre. Thai rices are delicate and lightly sticky, making them particularly good in stir-fries. Wild rice, which is actually an aquatic grass, has good levels of protein. Italian risotto rices have shorter grains and can absorb a great deal of liquid without becoming soggy, creating the desired creamy texture.

PASTA

The mainstay of many a cook in a hurry, pasta is also a good source of complex carbohydrates, and it is available in a multitude of shapes, colours and flavours. Pasta should be cooked until it is tender, but still firm to the bite. Choose pasta that is made from durum wheat or durum semolina. Cook it in plenty of lightly salted boiling water, according to the packet instructions, and drain well.

PULSES

Over half the world's main source of protein comes from pulses in one form or another. However, although high in protein, pulses are not complete in all amino acids. Grains, too, lack some amino acids, but by combining pulses and grains, you can complete the protein circle.

Dried pulses benefit from being soaked in cold water overnight. A shortcut is to cover them with boiling water and soak for 2 hours. Drain and cook in fresh water. Boil pulses vigorously for the first 10 minutes of cooking to destroy naturally occurring toxins. Then lower the heat and gently simmer. Do not add salt or lemon juice during cooking, as this toughens the skins, although herbs and perhaps slices of onion will add flavour. Drain the cooked pulses, but do not dry out completely.

Certain lentils can be cooked without pre-soaking. The small, split red lentils, masoor dhal, are marvellous for sprinkling in as thickeners for soups and stews and take just 20 minutes to cook. Beans with a good creamy texture that is perfect for soups, pâtés and purées are butter beans, kidney beans, cannellini, haricot, borlotti, pinto and flageolets. Split peas and red lentils make good dips. Chick-peas and aduki beans hold their texture well during cooking and make a good base for burgers and stews.

CHEESE

This is popular high-protein food with vegetarians, although not, of course, with vegans who do not eat dairy products. It is very high in calories compared with many other carbohydrate and protein foods. As it is so easy to incorporate in the vegetarian diet, there is a temptation to use it quite heavily and it is important to watch the intake of this potentially high cholesterol product.

For fuller flavour, choose well-matured varieties of cheese, such as mature farmhouse Cheddar or fresh Parmesan – you will then not need to use so much. Choose mature cheese for cooking. Leave some full-flavoured cheese unwrapped in the refrigerator to dry out: this concentrates the flavour and makes it go further when it is finely grated.

Among the most useful cheeses are

mature Cheddar, fresh Parmesan, mature Gruyère and pecorino. Lower fat soft cheese and goats' cheeses are ideal for stirring into hot food to make an instant, tasty, creamy sauce.

OTHER DAIRY PRODUCTS

Supermarkets carry a wide range of cultured dairy goods, which present many exciting opportunities to the home cook. Crème fraîche is a French-style soured cream which does not curdle when boiled, so it is ideal stirred into hot dishes. However, like double cream, it is quite high in fat (40 per cent), so use it sparingly.

Fromage frais and yogurt are smooth, slightly tangy, lower-fat, creamy products that are ideal for dressings and baked potatoes.

Curd, cream and cottage cheeses are long-time favourites and are now available in lower-fat versions.

DAIRY-FREE PRODUCTS

The unassuming soya bean is one of the best sources of high vegetable protein foods. It is ideal as a base for dairy-free milks, creams, spreads and cheeses, making it perfect for vegans and those with dairy product allergies. Use these products in the same way as their dairy product counterparts, although anyone coming newly to them will find that soy products taste slightly sweeter.

Tofu, also known as bean curd, is made with soy milk and is particularly versatile in vegetarian cooking, both as a main ingredient in recipes or to add creamy, firm texture. On its own, tofu has little flavour, making it ideal to use as an absorber of other flavours. This is

why it is so popular in Asian cooking. Firm tofu or bean curd can be cut into cubes, marinated or smoked. It is very good fried in oil or grilled to a crisp, golden crust.

A softer set tofu, called silken tofu, is a good substitute for cream in cooking and can be stirred into hot soups and used as a base filling for baked flans. Indeed, any time when a recipe calls for milk or cream, tofu can be used instead.

Not only high in protein, tofu is a good source of iron and vitamins of the B group. (Remember to serve some vitamin C during the same meal to enable the body to make · use of a vegetable source of iron.)

Mycoprotein (brand name Quorn) is a man-made food, distantly related to the mushroom. Low in fat and calories, it is high in protein and has as much fibre as green vegetables. It cooks quickly, absorbing flavours as easily as soya bean curd, but has a firmer texture. It is good for stir-frying, stews and casseroles.

NUTS AND SEEDS

Not only are they full of flavour, texture and colour, but nuts and seeds are great nutritional power packs. However, they can be high in fats as well as proteins.

Cheapest and most versatile are peanuts, which are best bought unsalted. Almonds are also very

useful, as are walnuts, pine nuts, hazelnuts and the more expensive cashews. Mixing two or three types together can be very successful.

Nuts go rancid if they are stored for more than about six months, so if you do not use them regularly, buy only small quantities. For maximum flavour, lightly roast nuts before chopping or crushing.

An increasing range of seeds is now available from supermarkets and wholefood stores. Most useful are sunflower and sesame seeds, while pumpkin and melon seeds are very attractive scattered into salads or nibbled with pre-dinner drinks. Seeds for an attractive garnish as well as flavour include poppy, black mustard, fenugreek and caraway seeds.

HERBS

Whenever possible, try to use fresh herbs. Do not use just one herb per dish: mix and match, experimenting with different combinations. Although you should not skimp on herbs, the more pungent ones, such as tarragon, rosemary and sage, should be used with discretion. Particularly useful herbs are parsley, coriander, dill, basil, chives and mint. If you have to use dried herbs, buy small quantities.

SOUPS &
STARTERS
~

PEAR AND WATERCRESS SOUP WITH STILTON CROÛTONS

PEARS AND STILTON TASTE VERY GOOD WHEN EATEN TOGETHER AFTER THE MAIN COURSE. HERE, FOR A CHANGE, THEY ARE COMBINED IN A STARTER.

SERVES SIX

INGREDIENTS
  1 bunch watercress
  4 medium pears, sliced
  900ml/1½ pints/3¾ cups vegetable
    stock
  salt and pepper
  120ml/4fl oz/½ cup double cream
  juice of 1 lime
For the croûtons
  25g/1oz butter
  15ml/1 tbsp olive oil
  200g/7oz/3 cups stale bread, cubed
  140g/5oz/1 cup Stilton cheese,
    chopped

1 Keep back about one-third of the watercress leaves. Place all the rest of the leaves and the stalks in a pan with the pears, stock and a little seasoning. Simmer for about 15–20 minutes. Reserving a few watercress leaves for garnish, add the rest and immediately blend in a food processor until smooth.

2 Put the mixture into a bowl and stir in the cream and lime juice to mix the flavours thoroughly. Season again to taste. Pour all the soup back into a pan and reheat, stirring until warmed through.

3 To make the croûtons, melt the butter and oil in a pan and fry the bread cubes until golden brown. Drain on kitchen paper. Put the cheese on top, then heat under a hot grill until bubbling.

4 Pour the reheated soup into bowls. Use the croûtons and remaining watercress leaves to garnish the soup before serving.

ASPARAGUS SOUP

HOME-MADE ASPARAGUS SOUP HAS A DELICATE FLAVOUR, QUITE UNLIKE THAT FROM A CAN. THIS SOUP IS BEST MADE WITH YOUNG ASPARAGUS, WHICH IS TENDER AND BLENDS WELL. SERVE IT WITH WAFER-THIN SLICES OF BREAD.

SERVES FOUR

INGREDIENTS
  450g/1lb young asparagus
  40g/1½ oz butter
  6 shallots, sliced
  15g/½ oz plain flour
  600ml/1 pint/2½ cups vegetable
    stock or water
  15ml/1 tbsp lemon juice
  250ml/8fl oz/1 cup milk
  120ml/4fl oz/½ cup single cream
  10ml/2 tsp chopped fresh chervil
  salt and freshly ground black pepper

1 Trim the stalks of the asparagus if necessary. Cut 4cm/1½in off the tops of half the asparagus and set aside for a garnish. Slice the remaining asparagus.

2 Melt 25g/1oz of the butter in a large saucepan and gently fry the sliced shallots for 2–3 minutes until soft but not brown, stirring occasionally.

3 Add the sliced asparagus and fry over a gentle heat for about 1 minute. Stir in the flour and cook for 1 minute. Stir in the stock or water and lemon juice and season to taste. Bring to the boil and then simmer, partially covered, for 15–20 minutes until the asparagus is very tender.

4 Cool slightly and then process the soup in a food processor or blender until smooth. Then press the puréed asparagus through a sieve placed over a clean saucepan. Add the milk by pouring and stirring it through the sieve with the asparagus so as to extract the maximum amount of asparagus purée.

5 Melt the remaining butter and fry the reserved asparagus tips gently for about 3–4 minutes to soften.

6 Heat the soup gently for 3–4 minutes. Stir in the cream and the asparagus tips. Continue to heat gently and serve sprinkled with the chopped fresh chervil.

CLASSIC MINESTRONE

THE HOME-MADE VERSION OF THIS FAMOUS SOUP IS A DELICIOUS REVELATION AND MOUTH-WATERINGLY HEALTHY.

SERVES FOUR

INGREDIENTS
1 large leek, thinly sliced
2 carrots, chopped
1 courgette, thinly sliced
115g/4oz whole green beans, halved
2 sticks celery, thinly sliced
45ml/3 tbsp olive oil
1.5 litres/2½ pints/6¼ cups stock
1 × 400g/14oz can chopped tomatoes
15ml/1 tbsp fresh basil, chopped
5ml/1 tsp fresh thyme leaves, chopped
  or 2.5ml/½ tsp dried thyme
salt and ground black pepper
1 × 400g/14oz can cannellini or kidney
  beans
50g/2oz/⅓ cup small pasta shapes or
  macaroni
fresh Parmesan cheese, finely grated
  (optional) and fresh parsley, chopped,
  to garnish

1 Put all the fresh vegetables into a large saucepan with the olive oil. Heat until sizzling, then cover, lower the heat and sweat the vegetables for 15 minutes, shaking the pan occasionally.

2 Add the stock (use water if you wish), tomatoes, herbs and seasoning. Bring to the boil, replace the lid and simmer gently for about 30 minutes.

3 Add the beans and their liquor together with the pasta, and simmer for a further 10 minutes. Check the seasoning and serve hot sprinkled with the Parmesan cheese (if used) and parsley.

COOK'S TIP
Minestrone is also delicious served cold on a hot summer's day. In fact, the flavour improves if it is made a day or two ahead and stored in the refrigerator. It can also be frozen and reheated.

GAZPACHO

Gazpacho is a classic Spanish soup. It is popular all over Spain but nowhere more so than in Andalucia, where there are hundreds of variations. It is a cold soup of tomatoes, tomato juice, green pepper and garlic, which is served with a selection of garnishes.

SERVES FOUR

INGREDIENTS

1.5kg/3–3½lb ripe tomatoes
1 green pepper, seeded and roughly
  chopped
2 garlic cloves, crushed
2 slices white bread, crusts removed
60ml/4 tbsp olive oil
60ml/4 tbsp tarragon wine vinegar
150ml/¼ pint/⅔ cup tomato juice
good pinch of sugar
salt and freshly ground black pepper
ice cubes, to serve

For the garnishes

30ml/2 tbsp sunflower oil
2–3 slices white bread, diced
1 small cucumber, peeled and
  finely diced
1 small onion, finely chopped
1 red pepper, seeded and finely diced
1 green pepper, seeded and finely
  diced
2 hard-boiled eggs, chopped

1 Skin the tomatoes, then quarter them and remove the cores.

2 Place the pepper in a food processor and process for a few seconds. Add the tomatoes, garlic, bread, olive oil and vinegar and process again. Add the tomato juice, sugar, seasoning and a little extra tomato juice or cold water and process. The consistency should be thick but not too stodgy.

3 Pour into a bowl and chill for at least 2 hours but no more than 12 hours, otherwise the textures deteriorate.

4 To prepare the bread cubes to use as a garnish, heat the oil in a frying pan and fry them over a moderate heat for 4-5 minutes until golden brown. Drain well on kitchen paper.

5 Place each garnish in a separate small dish, or alternatively arrange them in rows on a large plate.

6 Just before serving, stir a few ice cubes into the soup and then spoon into serving bowls. Serve with the garnishes.

WINTER WARMER SOUP

SIMMER A SELECTION OF POPULAR WINTER ROOT VEGETABLES TOGETHER FOR A WARMING AND SATISFYING SOUP.

SERVES SIX

INGREDIENTS
3 medium carrots, chopped
1 large potato, chopped
1 large parsnip, chopped
1 large turnip or small swede, chopped
1 onion, chopped
30ml/2 tbsp sunflower oil
25g/1oz/2 tbsp butter
1.5 litres/2½ pints/6 cups water
salt and ground black pepper
1 piece fresh root ginger, grated
300ml/½ pint/1¼ cups milk
45ml/3 tbsp crème fraîche, fromage
  frais or natural yogurt
30ml/2 tbsp fresh dill, chopped
fresh lemon juice

1 Put the carrots, potato, parsnip, turnip or swede and onion into a large saucepan with the oil and butter. Fry lightly, then cover and sweat the vegetables on a very low heat for 15 minutes, shaking the pan occasionally.

2 Pour in the water, bring to a boil and season well. Cover and simmer for 20 minutes until the vegetables are soft.

3 Strain the vegetables, reserving the stock, add the ginger and purée in a food processor or blender until smooth.

4 Return the purée and stock to the pan. Add the milk and stir while the soup gently reheats.

5 Remove from the heat, stir in the crème fraîche, fromage frais or yogurt plus the dill, lemon juice and extra seasoning, if necessary. Reheat the soup, if you wish, but do not allow it to boil as you do so, or it may curdle.

GARLIC MUSHROOMS

GARLIC AND MUSHROOMS MAKE A WONDERFUL COMBINATION. THEY MUST BE SERVED PIPING HOT, SO IF POSSIBLE USE A BALTI PAN OR CAST IRON FRYING PAN AND DON'T STAND ON CEREMONY — SERVE STRAIGHT FROM THE PAN.

SERVES FOUR

INGREDIENTS
    30ml/2 tbsp sunflower oil
    25g/1oz butter
    5 spring onions, thinly sliced
    3 garlic cloves, crushed
    450g/1lb button mushrooms
    40g/1½oz fresh white breadcrumbs
    15ml/1 tbsp chopped fresh parsley
    30ml/2 tbsp lemon juice
    salt and freshly ground black pepper

1 Heat the oil and butter in a balti pan, wok or cast iron frying pan. Add the spring onions and garlic and stir-fry over a medium heat for 1–2 minutes.

2 Add the whole button mushrooms and fry over a high heat for 4–5 minutes, stirring and tossing with a large wide spatula or wooden spoon, all the time.

3 Stir in the breadcrumbs, parsley, lemon juice and seasoning. Stir-fry for a few minutes until the lemon juice has virtually evaporated and then serve.

ROAST GARLIC WITH CROÛTONS

YOUR GUESTS WILL BE ASTONISHED TO BE SERVED A WHOLE ROAST GARLIC FOR A STARTER. ROAST GARLIC HAS A HEAVENLY FLAVOUR AND IS SO IRRESISTIBLE THAT THEY WILL EVEN FORGIVE YOU THE NEXT DAY!

SERVES FOUR

INGREDIENTS
    2 garlic bulbs
    45ml/3 tbsp olive oil
    45ml/3 tbsp water
    sprig of rosemary
    sprig of thyme
    1 bay leaf
    sea salt and freshly ground
       black pepper
To serve
    slices of French bread
    olive or sunflower oil, for frying
    175g/6oz young goat's cheese or soft
       cream cheese
    10ml/2 tsp chopped fresh herbs, e.g.
       marjoram, parsley and chives

3 Heat a little oil in a frying pan and fry the French bread on both sides until golden. Blend the cheese with the mixed herbs and place in a serving dish.

1 Preheat the oven to 190°C/375°F/ Gas 5. Place the garlic bulbs in a small ovenproof dish and pour over the oil and water. Add the rosemary, thyme and bay leaf and sprinkle with sea salt and pepper. Cover with foil and bake in the oven for 30 minutes.

2 Remove the foil, baste the garlic heads with the juices from the dish and bake for a further 15–20 minutes until they feel soft when pressed.

4 Cut each garlic bulb in half and open out slightly. Serve the garlic on small plates with the croûtons and soft cheese. Each garlic clove should be squeezed out of its papery shell, spread over a croûton and eaten with the cheese.

GUACAMOLE

THIS IS QUITE A FIERY VERSION OF A POPULAR MEXICAN DISH, ALTHOUGH PROBABLY NOWHERE NEAR AS HOT AS YOU WOULD BE SERVED IN MEXICO, WHERE IT SEEMS HEAT KNOWS NO BOUNDS!

SERVES FOUR

INGREDIENTS

2 ripe avocados, peeled and stoned
2 tomatoes, peeled, seeded and finely
  chopped
6 spring onions, finely chopped
1–2 chillies, seeded and finely
  chopped
30ml/2 tbsp fresh lime or lemon juice
15ml/1 tbsp chopped fresh coriander
salt and freshly ground black pepper
coriander sprigs, to garnish

1 Put the avocado halves into a large bowl and mash them roughly with a large fork.

2 Add the remaining ingredients. Mix well and season according to taste. Serve garnished with fresh coriander.

ROCKET AND GRILLED CHÈVRE SALAD

FOR THIS RECIPE, LOOK OUT FOR CYLINDER-SHAPED GOAT'S CHEESE FROM A DELICATESSEN OR FOR SMALL ROLLS THAT CAN BE CUT INTO HALVES, WEIGHING ABOUT 50G/2OZ. SERVE ONE PER PERSON AS A STARTER OR DOUBLE THE RECIPE AND SERVE TWO EACH FOR A LIGHT LUNCH.

SERVES FOUR

INGREDIENTS
    about 15ml/1 tbsp olive oil
    about 15ml/1 tbsp vegetable oil
    4 slices French bread
    45ml/3 tbsp walnut oil
    15ml/1 tbsp lemon juice
    salt and freshly ground black pepper
    225g/8oz cylinder-shaped goat's
        cheese
    generous handful of rocket leaves
    about 115g/4oz curly endive
For the sauce
    45ml/3 tbsp apricot jam
    60ml/4 tbsp white wine
    5ml/2 tsp Dijon mustard

1 Heat the two oils in a frying pan and fry the slices of French bread on one side only, until lightly golden. Transfer to a plate lined with kitchen paper.

4 Preheat the grill a few minutes before serving the salad. Cut the goat's cheese into 50g/2oz rounds and place each piece on a croûton, untoasted side up. Place under the grill and cook for 3–4 minutes until the cheese melts.

5 Toss the rocket and curly endive in the walnut oil dressing and arrange attractively on four individual serving plates. When the cheese croûtons are ready, arrange on each plate and pour over a little of the apricot sauce.

2 To make the sauce, heat the jam in a small saucepan until warm but not boiling. Push through a sieve, into a clean pan, to remove the pieces of fruit, and then stir in the white wine and mustard. Heat gently and keep warm until ready to serve.

3 Blend the walnut oil and lemon juice and season with a little salt and pepper.

MUSHROOMS ON TOAST

*SERVE THESE ON TOAST FOR A
QUICK, TASTY STARTER OR POP
THEM INTO SMALL RAMEKINS AND
SERVE WITH SLICES OF WARM
CRUSTY BREAD. USE SOME
SHITAKE MUSHROOMS, IF YOU
CAN FIND THEM, FOR A RICHER
FLAVOUR.*

SERVES FOUR

INGREDIENTS
    450g/1lb button mushrooms, sliced if
        large
    45ml/3 tbsp olive oil
    45ml/3 tbsp stock or water
    30ml/2 tbsp dry sherry (optional)
    3 garlic cloves, crushed
    115g/4oz low fat soft cheese
    30ml/2 tbsp fresh parsley, chopped
    15ml/1 tbsp fresh chives, chopped
    salt and ground black pepper

1 Put the mushrooms into a large
saucepan with the olive oil, stock or water
and sherry, if using. Heat until bubbling
then cover and simmer for 5 minutes.

2 Add the garlic and stir well. Cook for a
further 2 minutes. Remove the
mushrooms with a slotted spoon and set
them aside. Cook the liquor until it
reduces down to 30ml/2 tbsp. Remove
from the heat and stir in the cheese and
herbs.

3 Stir the mixture well until the cheese
melts, then return the mushrooms to the
pan so that they become coated with the
cheesy mixture. Season to taste.

4 Pile the mushrooms onto thick slabs of
hot toast. Alternatively, spoon them into
four ramekins and serve accompanied by
slices of crusty bread.

RICOTTA AND BORLOTTI BEAN PÂTÉ

*FOR AN ATTRACTIVE
PRESENTATION, SPOON THE PÂTÉ
INTO SMALL, OILED RING
MOULDS, TURN OUT AND FILL
WITH WHOLE BORLOTTI BEANS,
DRESSED WITH LEMON JUICE,
OLIVE OIL AND FRESH HERBS.*

SERVES FOUR

INGREDIENTS
    1 × 400g/14oz can borlotti beans,
        drained
    1 garlic clove, crushed
    175g/6oz ricotta cheese (or other
        cream cheese)
    50g/2oz/4 tbsp butter, melted
    juice of ½ lemon
    salt and ground black pepper
    30ml/2 tbsp fresh parsley, chopped
    15ml/1 tbsp fresh thyme or dill,
        chopped
To serve
    extra canned beans (optional)
    fresh lemon juice, olive oil and
        chopped herbs (optional)
    salad leaves, radish slices and a few
        sprigs fresh dill, to garnish

1 Blend the beans, garlic, cheese, butter,
lemon juice and seasoning in a food
processor until smooth.

2 Add the chopped herbs and continue
to blend. Spoon into one serving dish or
four lightly oiled ramekins, the bases lined
with discs of non-stick baking paper. Chill
the pâté so that it sets firm.

3 If serving with extra beans, dress them
with lemon juice, olive oil and herbs,
season well and spoon on top. Garnish
with salad leaves and serve with warm
crusty bread or toast.

4 If serving individually, turn each pâté
out of its ramekin onto a small plate and
remove the disc of paper. Top with radish
slices and sprigs of dill.

VARIATION
You could try other canned pulses for this
recipe, although the softer lentils would
not be suitable. Butter (lima) beans are
surprisingly good. For an attractive
presentation, fill the centre with dark red
kidney beans and chopped fresh green
beans.

ARTICHOKES WITH GARLIC AND HERB BUTTER

IT IS FUN EATING ARTICHOKES AND EVEN MORE FUN TO SHARE ONE BETWEEN TWO PEOPLE. YOU CAN ALWAYS HAVE A SECOND ONE TO FOLLOW SO THAT YOU GET YOUR FAIR SHARE!

SERVES FOUR

INGREDIENTS
2 large or 4 medium globe artichokes
salt
For the garlic and herb butter
75g/3oz butter
1 garlic clove, crushed
15ml/1 tbsp mixed chopped fresh
tarragon, marjoram and parsley

1 Wash the artichokes well in cold water. Using a sharp knife, cut off the stalks level with the bases. Cut off the top 1cm/½in of leaves. Snip off the pointed ends of the remaining leaves with scissors.

2 Put the prepared artichokes in a large saucepan of lightly salted water. Bring to the boil, cover and cook for about 40–45 minutes or until a lower leaf comes away easily when gently pulled.

3 Drain upside down for a couple of minutes while making the sauce. Melt the butter over a low heat, add the garlic and cook for 30 seconds. Remove from the heat, stir in the herbs and then pour into one or two small serving bowls.

4 Place the artichokes on serving plates and serve with the garlic and herb butter.

COOK'S TIP
To eat an artichoke, pull off each leaf and dip into the garlic and herb butter. Scrape off the soft fleshy base with your teeth. When the centre is reached, pull out the hairy choke and discard it, as it is inedible. The base can be cut up and eaten with the remaining garlic butter.

PLANTAIN APPETIZER

*PLANTAINS ARE A TYPE OF COOKING BANANA WITH A LOWER SUGAR CONTENT THAN DESSERT BANANAS.
THEY ARE UNSUITABLE FOR EATING RAW BUT CAN BE USED IN A WIDE RANGE OF DISHES. THIS
DELICIOUS ASSORTMENT OF SWEET AND SAVOURY PLANTAINS IS A POPULAR DISH IN AFRICA.*

SERVES FOUR

INGREDIENTS
2 green plantains
45ml/3 tbsp vegetable oil
1 small onion, very thinly sliced
1 yellow plantain
½ garlic clove, crushed
salt and cayenne pepper
vegetable oil, for frying

1 Peel one of the green plantains and
cut into wafer-thin rounds, preferably
using a swivel-headed potato peeler.

2 Heat about 15ml/1 tbsp of the oil in a
large frying pan and fry the plantain
slices for 2–3 minutes until golden,
turning occasionally. Transfer to a plate
lined with kitchen paper and keep warm.

3 Coarsely grate the other green
plantain and mix with the onion.

4 Heat 15ml/1 tbsp of the remaining oil
in the pan and fry the plantain and onion
mixture for 2–3 minutes until golden,
turning occasionally. Transfer to the plate
with the plantain slices.

5 Peel the yellow plantain, cut into small
chunks. Sprinkle with cayenne pepper.
Heat the remaining oil and fry the yellow
plantain and garlic for 4–5 minutes until
brown. Drain and sprinkle with salt.

MEDITERRANEAN VEGETABLES <u>WITH</u> TAHINI

WONDERFULLY COLOURFUL, THIS STARTER IS EASILY PREPARED IN ADVANCE. TAHINI IS A PASTE MADE FROM SESAME SEEDS.

SERVES FOUR

INGREDIENTS
  2 peppers, seeded and quartered
  2 courgettes, halved lengthways
  2 small aubergines, degorged and
    halved lengthways
  1 fennel bulb, quartered
  olive oil
  salt and ground black pepper
  115g/4oz Greek Halloumi cheese,
    sliced
For the tahini cream
  225g/8oz/1 cup tahini paste
  1 garlic cloves, crushed
  30ml/2 tbsp olive oil
  30ml/2 tbsp fresh lemon juice
  120ml/4 floz/½ cup cold water

1 Preheat the grill or barbecue until hot. Brush the vegetables with the oil and grill until just browned, turning once. (If the peppers blacken, don't worry. The skins can be peeled off.) Cook the vegetables until just softened.

2 Place the vegetables in a shallow dish and season. Allow to cool. Meanwhile, brush the cheese slices with oil and grill these on both sides until just charred. Remove them with a palette knife.

3 To make the tahini cream, place all the ingredients, except the water, in a food processor or blender. Whizz for a few seconds to mix, then, with the motor still running, pour in the water and blend until smooth.

4 Serve the vegetables and cheese on a platter and trickle over the cream. Delicious served with warm pitta or naan bread.

COOK'S TIP
To degorge aubergines, sprinkle cut slices with salt and allow the juices that form to drain away in a colander. After 30 minutes or so, rinse well and pat dry. Degorged aubergines are less bitter and easier to cook.

DOLMADES

DOLMADES ARE STUFFED VINE LEAVES, A TRADITIONAL GREEK DISH. IF YOU CAN'T OBTAIN FRESH VINE LEAVES, USE A PACKET OF BRINED VINE LEAVES. SOAK THE LEAVES IN HOT WATER FOR 20 MINUTES THEN RINSE AND DRY WELL ON KITCHEN PAPER BEFORE USE.

MAKES 20–24

INGREDIENTS

  20–30 fresh young vine leaves
  30ml/2 tbsp olive oil
  1 large onion, finely chopped
  1 garlic clove, crushed
  225g/8oz cooked long grain rice,
    or mixed white and wild rice
  about 45ml/3 tbsp pine nuts
  15ml/1 tbsp flaked almonds
  40g/1½oz sultanas
  15ml/ 1 tbsp snipped chives
  15ml/ 1 tbsp finely chopped
    fresh mint
  juice of ½ lemon
  150ml/¼ pint/⅔ cup white wine
  hot vegetable stock
  salt and freshly ground black pepper
  sprig of mint, to garnish
  Greek yogurt, to serve

1 Bring a large pan of water to the boil and cook the vine leaves for about 2–3 minutes. They will darken and go limp after about 1 minute and simmering for a further minute or so ensures they are pliable. If using leaves from a packet, place them in a large bowl, cover with boiling water and leave for a few minutes until the leaves can be easily separated. Rinse them under cold water and drain on kitchen paper.

2 Heat the oil in a small frying pan and fry the onion and garlic for 3–4 minutes over a gentle heat until soft.

3 Spoon the onion and garlic mixture into a bowl and add the cooked rice.

4 Stir in 30ml/2 tbsp of the pine nuts, the almonds, sultanas, chives, mint, lemon juice and seasoning and mix well.

5 Lay a vine leaf on a clean work surface, veined side uppermost. Place a spoonful of filling near the stem, fold the lower part of the leaf over it and roll up, folding in the sides as you go. Continue stuffing the vine leaves in the same way.

6 Line the base of a deep frying pan with four large vine leaves. Place the stuffed vine leaves close together in the pan, seam side down, in a single layer.

7 Add the wine and enough stock to just cover the vine leaves. Place a plate directly over the leaves, then cover and simmer gently for 30 minutes, checking to make sure the pan does not boil dry.

8 Chill the vine leaves, then serve garnished with the remaining pine nuts, a sprig of mint and a little yogurt.

BRUSCHETTA WITH GOATS' CHEESE AND TAPENADE

*SIMPLE TO PREPARE IN ADVANCE,
THIS APPETIZING DISH CAN BE
SERVED AS A STARTER OR AT
FINGER BUFFETS.*

SERVES FOUR TO SIX

INGREDIENTS
For the tapenade
  1 × 400g/14oz can black olives, stoned
    and finely chopped
  50g/2oz sun-dried tomatoes in oil,
    chopped
  30ml/2 tbsp capers, chopped
  15ml/1 tbsp green peppercorns, in
    brine, crushed
  45–60ml/3–4 tbsp olive oil
  2 garlic cloves, crushed
  45ml/3 tbsp fresh basil, chopped, or
  5ml/1 tsp dried basil
  salt and ground black pepper
For the bases
  12 slices ciabatta or other crusty bread
  olive oil, for brushing
  2 garlic cloves, halved
  115g/4oz soft goats' cheese
  fresh herb sprigs, to garnish

1 Mix the tapenade ingredients all together and check the seasoning. It should not need too much. Allow to marinate overnight, if possible.

2 To make the bruschetta, grill both sides of the bread lightly until golden. Brush one side with oil and then rub with a cut clove of garlic. Set aside until ready to serve.

3 Spread the bruschetta with the cheese, roughing it up with a fork, and spoon the tapenade on top. Garnish with sprigs of herbs.

COOK'S TIP
The bruschetta is nicest grilled over a open barbecue flame, if possible. Failing that, a grill will do, but avoid using a toaster – it gives too even a colour and the bruschetta is supposed to look quite rustic.

WARM AVOCADOS WITH TANGY TOPPING

*LIGHTLY GRILLED WITH A TASTY
TOPPING OF RED ONIONS AND
CHEESE, THIS MAKES A DELIGHTFUL
ALTERNATIVE TO THE RATHER
HUMDRUM AVOCADO VINAIGRETTE.*

SERVES FOUR

INGREDIENTS
  1 small red onion, sliced
  1 garlic clove, crushed
  15ml/1 tbsp sunflower oil
  soy sauce
  2 ripe avocados, halved and stoned
  2 small tomatoes, sliced
  15ml/1 tbsp fresh chopped basil,
    marjoram or parsley
  50g/2oz Lancashire or Mozzarella
    cheese, sliced
  salt and ground black pepper

1 Gently fry the onion and garlic in the oil for about 5 minutes until just softened. Shake in a little soy sauce.

2 Preheat a grill. Place the avocado halves on the grill pan and spoon the onions into the centre.

3 Divide the tomato slices and fresh herbs between the four halves and top each one with the cheese.

4 Season well and grill until the cheese melts and starts to brown.

VARIATION
Avocados are wonderful served in other hot dishes too. Try them chopped and tossed into hot pasta or sliced and layered in a lasagne.

LIGHT
MEALS

MACARONI SOUFFLÉ

*THIS IS GENERALLY A GREAT
FAVOURITE WITH CHILDREN, AND
IS RATHER LIKE A LIGHT AND
FLUFFY MACARONI CHEESE.*

<u>SERVES THREE TO FOUR</u>

INGREDIENTS
75g/3oz short cut macaroni
melted butter, to coat
25g/1oz/3 tbsp dried breadcrumbs
50g/2oz/4 tbsp butter
5ml/1 tsp ground paprika
40g/1½oz/⅓ cup plain flour
300ml/½ pint/1¼ cups milk
75g/3oz Cheddar or Gruyère cheese,
    grated
50g/2oz Parmesan cheese, grated
salt and ground black pepper
3 eggs, separated

1 Boil the macaroni according to the
instructions on the pack. Drain well and
then set aside. Preheat the oven to
150°C/300°F/Gas 2.

2 Brush the insides of a 1.2 litre/2 pint
soufflé dish with melted butter, then coat
evenly with the breadcrumbs, shaking out
any excess.

3 Put the butter, paprika, flour and milk
into a saucepan and bring to the boil
slowly, whisking it constantly until it is
smooth and thick.

4 Simmer the sauce for a minute, then
take off the heat and stir in the cheeses
until they melt. Season well and mix with
the macaroni.

5 Beat in the egg yolks. Whisk the egg
whites until they form soft peaks and
spoon a quarter into the sauce mixture,
beating it gently to loosen it up.

6 Using a large metal spoon, carefully
fold in the rest of the egg whites and
transfer to the prepared soufflé dish.

7 Bake in the centre of the oven for
about 40–45 minutes until the soufflé has
risen and is golden brown. The middle
should wobble very slightly and the soufflé
should be lightly creamy inside.

ADUKI BEAN BURGERS

ALTHOUGH NOT QUICK TO MAKE, THESE ARE A DELICIOUS ALTERNATIVE TO SHOP-BOUGHT BURGERS.

MAKES 12

INGREDIENTS
  200g/7oz/1 cup brown rice
  1 onion, chopped
  2 garlic cloves, crushed
  30ml/2 tbsp sunflower oil
  50g/2oz/4 tbsp butter
  1 small green pepper, seeded and chopped
  1 carrot, coarsely grated
  1 × 400g/14oz can aduki beans, drained (or 125g/4oz dried weight, soaked and cooked)
  1 egg, beaten
  125g/4oz mature cheese, grated
  5ml/1 tsp dried thyme
  50g/2oz/½ cup roasted hazelnuts or toasted flaked almonds
  salt and ground black pepper
  wholemeal flour or cornmeal, for coating
  oil, for deep frying

1 Cook the rice according to the instructions on the pack, allowing it to slightly overcook so that it is softer. Strain the rice and transfer it to a large bowl.

2 Fry the onion and garlic in the oil and butter together with the green pepper and carrot for about 10 minutes until the vegetables are softened.

3 Mix this vegetable mixture into the rice, together with the aduki beans, egg, cheese, thyme, nuts or almonds and plenty of seasoning. Chill until quite firm.

4 Shape into 12 patties, using wet hands if the mixture sticks. Coat the patties in flour or cornmeal and set aside.

5 Heat 1cm/½in oil in a large, shallow frying pan and fry the burgers in batches until browned on each side, about five minutes in total. Remove and drain on kitchen paper. Eat some burgers freshly cooked, and freeze the rest for later. Serve in buns with salad and relish.

COOK'S TIP
To freeze the burgers, cool them after cooking, then open freeze them before wrapping and bagging. Use within six weeks. Cook from frozen by baking in a pre-heated moderately hot oven for 20–25 minutes.

BALTI-STYLE CAULIFLOWER <u>WITH</u> TOMATOES

BALTI IS A TYPE OF MEAT AND VEGETABLE COOKING FROM PAKISTAN AND NORTHERN INDIA. IT CAN REFER BOTH TO THE PAN USED FOR COOKING, WHICH IS LIKE A LITTLE WOK, AND THE SPICES USED. IN THE ABSENCE OF A GENUINE BALTI PAN, USE EITHER A WOK OR A HEAVY FRYING PAN.

SERVES FOUR

INGREDIENTS

30ml/2 tbsp vegetable oil
1 onion, chopped
2 garlic cloves, crushed
1 cauliflower, broken into florets
5ml/1 tsp ground coriander
5ml/1 tsp ground cumin
5ml/1 tsp ground fennel seeds
2.5ml/½ tsp garam masala
pinch of ground ginger
2.5ml/½ tsp chilli powder
4 plum tomatoes, peeled, seeded
  and quartered
175ml/6fl oz/¾ cup water
175g/6oz fresh spinach, roughly
  chopped
15–30ml/1–2 tbsp lemon juice
salt and freshly ground black
  pepper

1 Heat the oil in a balti pan, wok, or large frying pan. Add the onion and garlic and stir-fry for 2–3 minutes over a high heat until the onion begins to brown. Add the cauliflower florets and stir-fry for a further 2–3 minutes until the cauliflower is flecked with brown.

2 Add the coriander, cumin, fennel seeds, garam masala, ginger and chilli powder and cook over a high heat for 1 minute, stirring all the time; then add the tomatoes, water and salt and pepper. Bring to the boil and then reduce the heat, cover and simmer for 5–6 minutes until the cauliflower is just tender.

3 Stir in the chopped spinach, cover and cook for 1 minute until the spinach is tender. Add enough lemon juice to sharpen the flavour and adjust the seasoning to taste.

4 Serve straight from the pan, with an Indian meal or with chicken or meat.

PARSNIP AND CHESTNUT CROQUETTES

THE SWEET NUTTY TASTE OF CHESTNUTS BLENDS PERFECTLY WITH THE SIMILARLY SWEET BUT EARTHY FLAVOUR OF PARSNIPS. FRESH CHESTNUTS NEED TO BE PEELED BUT FROZEN CHESTNUTS ARE EASY TO USE AND ARE NEARLY AS GOOD AS FRESH FOR THIS RECIPE.

MAKES TEN TO TWELVE

INGREDIENTS

 450g/1lb parsnips, cut roughly into
  small pieces
 115g/4oz frozen chestnuts
 25g/1oz butter
 1 garlic clove, crushed
 15ml/1tbsp chopped fresh coriander
 1 egg, beaten
 40–50g/1½–2oz fresh white
  breadcrumbs
 vegetable oil, for frying
 salt and freshly ground black pepper
 sprig of coriander, to garnish

1 Place the parsnips in a saucepan with enough water to cover. Bring to the boil, cover and simmer for 15–20 minutes until completely tender.

2 Place the frozen chestnuts in a pan of water, bring to the boil and simmer for 8–10 minutes until very tender. Drain, place in a bowl and mash roughly.

3 Melt the butter in a small saucepan and cook the garlic for 30 seconds. Drain the parsnips and mash with the garlic butter. Stir in the chestnuts and chopped coriander, then season well.

4 Take about 15ml/1tbsp of the mixture at a time and form into small croquettes, about 7.5cm/3in long. Dip each croquette into the beaten egg and then roll in the breadcrumbs.

5 Heat a little oil in a frying pan and fry the croquettes for 3–4 minutes until golden, turning frequently so they brown evenly. Drain on kitchen paper and then serve at once, garnished with coriander.

SPINACH AND PEPPER PIZZA

MAKES TWO 30cm/12in PIZZAS

INGREDIENTS
  450g/1lb fresh spinach
  60ml/4 tbsp single cream
  25g/1oz Parmesan cheese, grated
  15ml/1 tbsp olive oil
  1 large onion, chopped
  1 garlic clove, crushed
  ½ green pepper, seeded and thinly
    sliced
  ½ red pepper, seeded and thinly sliced
  175–250ml/6–8fl oz/¾-1 cup passata
    sauce or puréed tomatoes
  50g/2oz black olives, pitted and
    chopped
  15ml/1 tbsp chopped fresh basil
  175g/6oz mozzarella, grated
  175g/6oz Cheddar cheese, grated
  salt
For the dough
  25g/1oz fresh yeast or 15ml/1 tbsp
    dried yeast and 5ml/1 tsp sugar
  about 225ml/7fl oz/⅞ cup warm water
  350g/12oz strong white flour
  30ml/2 tbsp olive oil
  5ml/1 tsp salt

1 To make the dough, cream together the fresh yeast and 150ml/¼ pint/⅔ cup of the water and set aside until frothy. If using dried yeast, stir the sugar into 150ml/¼ pint/⅔ cup water, sprinkle over the yeast and leave until frothy.

2 Place the flour and salt in a large bowl, make a well in the centre and pour in the olive oil and yeast mixture. Add the remaining water, mix to make a stiff but pliable dough. Knead on a lightly floured surface for about 10 minutes until smooth and elastic.

3 Shape the dough into a ball and place in a lightly oiled bowl, cover with clear film and leave in a warm place for about 1 hour until it has doubled in size.

4 To prepare the topping, cook the spinach over a moderate heat for 4–5 minutes until the leaves have wilted. Strain and press out the excess liquid. Place in a bowl and mix with the cream, Parmesan cheese and salt to taste.

5 Heat the oil in a frying pan and fry the onion and garlic over a moderate heat for 3–4 minutes until the onion has slightly softened. Add the peppers and continue cooking until the onion is lightly golden, stirring regularly.

6 Preheat the oven to 220°C/425°F/ Gas 7. Knead the dough briefly on a lightly floured surface. Divide the dough and roll out into two 30cm/12in rounds.

7 Spread each base with the passata sauce or puréed tomatoes. Add the onions and peppers and then spread over the spinach mixture. Scatter the olives and basil leaves and sprinkle with the mozzarella and Cheddar cheese.

8 Bake in the oven for 15–20 minutes, or until the crust is lightly browned and the top is beginning to turn golden. Allow to cool slightly before serving.

ARTICHOKE RÖSTI

SERVES FOUR TO SIX

INGREDIENTS
    450g/1lb Jerusalem artichokes
    juice of 1 lemon
    450g/1lb potatoes
    about 50g/2oz butter
    salt

1 Peel the Jerusalem artichokes and place in a saucepan of water together with the lemon juice and a pinch of salt. Bring to the boil and cook for about 5 minutes until barely tender.

2 Peel the potatoes and place in a separate pan of salted water. Bring to the boil and cook until barely tender – they will take slightly longer than the artichokes.

3 Drain and cool both the artichokes and potatoes, and then grate them into a bowl. Mix them with your fingers, without breaking them up too much.

4 Melt the butter in a large heavy-based frying pan. Add the artichoke mixture, spreading it out with the back of a spoon. Cook gently for about 10 minutes.

5 Invert the "cake" on to a plate and slide back into the pan. Cook for about 10 minutes until golden. Serve at once.

ARTICHOKE TIMBALES WITH SPINACH SAUCE

SERVES SIX

INGREDIENTS
    900g/2lb Jerusalem artichokes
    juice of 1 lemon
    25g/1oz butter
    15ml/1 tbsp oil
    1 onion, finely chopped
    1 garlic clove, crushed
    50g/2oz fresh white breadcrumbs
    1 egg
    60–75ml/4–5 tbsp vegetable stock
        or milk
    15ml/1 tbsp chopped fresh parsley
    5ml/1 tsp finely chopped sage
    salt and freshly ground black pepper
For the sauce
    225g/8oz fresh spinach, prepared
    15g/½oz butter
    2 shallots, finely chopped
    150ml/¼ pint/⅔ cup single cream
    175ml/6fl oz/¾ cup vegetable stock
    salt and freshly ground black pepper

1 Preheat the oven to 180°C/350°F/ Gas 4. Grease six 150ml/¼ pint/⅔ cup ramekin dishes, and then place a circle of non-stick baking paper in each base.

2 Peel the artichokes and put in a saucepan with the lemon juice and water to cover. Bring to the boil and simmer for about 10 minutes until tender. Drain and mash with the butter.

3 Heat the oil in a small frying pan and fry the onion and garlic until soft. Place in a food processor with the breadcrumbs, egg, stock or milk, parsley, sage and seasoning. Process to a smooth purée, add the artichokes and process again briefly. Do not over-process.

4 Put the mixture in the prepared dishes and smooth the tops. Cover with non-stick baking paper, place in a roasting tin half-filled with boiling water and bake for 35–40 minutes until firm.

5 To make the sauce, cook the spinach without water, in a large covered saucepan, for 2–3 minutes. Shake the pan occasionally. Strain and press out the excess liquid.

6 Melt the butter in a small saucepan and fry the shallots gently until slightly softened but not browned. Place in a food processor or blender with the spinach and process to make a smooth purée. Pour back into the pan, add the cream and seasoning, and keep warm over a very low heat. Do not allow the mixture to boil.

7 Allow the timbales to stand for a few minutes after cooking and then turn out on to warmed serving plates. Spoon the warm sauce over them and serve.

COOK'S TIP
When puréeing the artichokes in a food processor or blender, use the pulse button and process for a very short time. The mixture will become cloying if it is over-processed.

STUFFED MUSHROOMS

THIS IS A CLASSIC MUSHROOM DISH, STRONGLY FLAVOURED WITH GARLIC. USE FLAT MUSHROOMS OR
FIELD MUSHROOMS THAT ARE SOMETIMES AVAILABLE FROM FARM SHOPS.

SERVES FOUR

INGREDIENTS
    450g/1lb large flat mushrooms
    butter, for greasing
    about 75ml/5 tbsp olive oil
    2 garlic cloves, minced or very
       finely chopped
    45ml/3 tbsp finely chopped fresh
       parsley
    40–50g/1½–2oz fresh white
       breadcrumbs
    salt and freshly ground black pepper
    sprig of flat leaf parsley, to garnsh

1 Preheat the oven to 180°C/350°F/
Gas 4. Cut off the mushroom stalks and
reserve on one side.

2 Arrange the mushroom caps in a
buttered shallow dish, gill side upwards.

COOK'S TIP
The cooking time for the mushrooms
depends on their size and thickness. If
they are fairly thin, cook for slightly less
time. They should be tender but not too
soft when cooked. If a stronger garlic
flavour is preferred, do not cook the
garlic before adding it to the breadcrumb
mixture.

3 Heat 15ml/1 tbsp of oil in a frying pan
and fry the garlic briefly. Finely chop the
mushroom stalks and mix with the parsley and breadcrumbs. Add the garlic,
seasoning and 15ml/1tbsp of the oil. Pile
a little of the mixture on each mushroom.

4 Add the remaining oil to the dish and
cover the mushrooms with buttered
greaseproof paper. Bake for about
15–20 minutes, removing the paper for
the last 5 minutes to brown the tops.
Garnish with a sprig of flat leaf parsley.

HOT SOUR CHICK-PEAS

THIS DISH, KHATTE CHOLE, IS EATEN AS A SNACK ALL OVER INDIA, SOLD BY ITINERANT STREET VENDORS. THE HEAT OF THE CHILLIES IS TEMPERED PARTLY BY THE CORIANDER AND CUMIN, WHILE THE LEMON JUICE ADDS A WONDERFUL SOURNESS.

SERVES FOUR

INGREDIENTS
    350g/12oz chick-peas, soaked
      overnight
    60ml/4 tbsp vegetable oil
    2 medium onions, very finely chopped
    225g/8oz tomatoes, peeled and finely
      chopped
    15ml/1 tbsp ground coriander
    15ml/1 tbsp ground cumin
    5ml/1 tsp ground fenugreek
    5ml/1 tsp ground cinnamon
    1–2 hot green chillies, seeded
      and finely sliced
    about 2.5cm/1in fresh root ginger,
      grated
    60ml/4 tbsp lemon juice
    15ml/1 tbsp chopped fresh coriander
    salt

1 Drain the chick-peas and place them in a large saucepan, cover with water and bring to the boil. Cover and simmer for 1–1¼ hours until tender, making sure the chick-peas do not boil dry. Drain, reserving the cooking liquid.

2 Heat the oil in a large flameproof casserole. Reserve about 30ml/2 tbsp of the chopped onions and fry the remainder in the casserole over a moderate heat for 4–5 minutes, stirring frequently, until tinged with brown.

3 Add the tomatoes and continue cooking over a moderately low heat for 5–6 minutes until soft. Stir frequently, mashing the tomatoes to a pulp.

4 Stir in the coriander, cumin, fenugreek and cinnamon. Cook for 30 seconds and then add the chick-peas and 350ml/12fl oz/1½ cups of the reserved cooking liquid. Season with salt, cover and simmer very gently for about 15–20 minutes, stirring occasionally and adding more cooking liquid if the mixture becomes too dry.

5 Meanwhile, mix the reserved onion with the chilli, ginger and lemon juice.

6 Just before serving, stir the onion and chilli mixture and the coriander into the chick-peas, and adjust the seasoning.

HOT BROCCOLI TARTLETS

IN FRANCE, HOME OF THE CLASSIC QUICHE LORRAINE, YOU CAN ALSO FIND A WHOLE VARIETY OF SAVOURY TARTLETS, FILLED WITH ONIONS, LEEKS, MUSHROOMS AND BROCCOLI. THIS VERSION IS SIMPLE TO PREPARE AND WOULD MAKE AN ELEGANT START TO A MEAL.

MAKES EIGHT TO TEN

INGREDIENTS
   15ml/1 tbsp oil
   1 leek, finely sliced
   175g/6oz broccoli, broken into florets
   15g/½oz butter
   15g/½oz plain flour
   150ml/¼ pint/⅔ cup milk
   50g/2oz goat's Cheddar or farmhouse
    Cheddar, grated
   fresh chervil, to garnish
For the pastry
   175g/6oz plain flour
   75g/3oz butter
   1 egg
   pinch of salt

1 To make the pastry, place the flour and salt in a large bowl and rub in the butter and egg to make a dough. Add a little cold water if necessary, knead lightly, then wrap in clear film and leave to rest in the fridge for 1 hour.

2 Preheat the oven to 190°C/375°F/Gas 5. Let the dough return to room temperature for 10 minutes and then roll out on a lightly floured surface and line 8–10 deep patty tins. Prick the bases with a fork and bake in the oven for about 10–15 minutes until the pastry is firm and lightly golden. Increase the oven temperature to 200°C/400°F/Gas 6.

3 Heat the oil in a small saucepan and sauté the leek for 4–5 minutes until soft. Add the broccoli, stir-fry for about 1 minute and then add a little water. Cover and steam for 3–4 minutes until the broccoli is just tender.

4 Melt the butter in a separate saucepan, stir in the flour and cook for a minute, stirring all the time. Slowly add the milk and stir to make a smooth sauce. Add half of the cheese and season with salt and pepper.

5 Spoon a little broccoli and leek into each tartlet case and then spoon over the sauce. Sprinkle each tartlet with the remaining cheese and then bake in the oven for about 10 minutes until golden.

6 Serve the tartlets as part of a buffet or as a starter, garnished with chervil.

CAULIFLOWER AND EGG CHEESE

A QUICK ALL-IN-ONE SAUCE CAN BE MADE IN MINUTES, WHILE A SMALL PACK OF SOUP CROÛTONS GIVES THE DISH A DELICIOUS CRUNCHY TOPPING.

<u>SERVES FOUR</u>

INGREDIENTS

   1 medium size cauliflower, in florets
   1 medium onion, sliced
   2 eggs, hard boiled, peeled and
     chopped
   40g/1½oz/3 tbsp wholemeal flour
   5ml/1 tsp mild curry powder
   25g/1oz/2 tbsp sunflower margarine or
     low-fat spread
   450ml/¾ pint/2 cups milk
   2.5ml/½ tsp dried thyme
   salt and ground black pepper
   115g/4oz mature cheese, grated
   small packet of soup croûtons

1 Boil the cauliflower and onion in enough salted water to cover until they are just tender. Be careful not to overcook them. Drain well.

2 Arrange the cauliflower and onion in a shallow ovenproof dish and scatter over the chopped egg.

3 Put the flour, curry powder, fat and milk in a saucepan all together. Bring slowly to the boil, stirring well until thickened and smooth. Stir in the thyme and seasoning and allow the sauce to simmer for a minute or two. Remove the pan from the heat and stir in about three quarters of the cheese.

4 Pour the sauce over the cauliflower, scatter over the croûtons and sprinkle with the remaining cheese. Brown under a hot grill until golden and serve. Delicious with thick crusty bread.

BAKED COURGETTES

When very small and very fresh courgettes are used for this recipe it is wonderful, both simple and delicious. The creamy yet tangy goat's cheese contrasts well with the very delicate flavour of the young courgettes.

SERVES FOUR

INGREDIENTS

   8 small courgettes, about 450g/1lb
     total weight
   15ml/1 tbsp olive oil, plus extra
     for greasing
   75–115g/3–4oz goat's cheese, cut
     into thin strips
   small bunch fresh mint, finely
     chopped
   freshly ground black pepper

1 Preheat the oven to 180°C/350°F/ Gas 4. Cut out eight rectangles of foil large enough to encase each courgette and brush each with a little oil.

2 Trim the courgettes and cut a thin slit along the length of each.

3 Insert pieces of goat's cheese in the slits. Add a little mint and sprinkle with the olive oil and black pepper.

4 Wrap each courgette in the foil rectangles, place on a baking sheet and bake for about 25 minutes until tender.

COOK'S TIP
Almost any cheese could be used in this recipe. Mild cheeses, however, such as a mild cheddar or mozzarella, will best allow the flavour of the courgettes to be appreciated.

KITCHIRI

THIS IS THE INDIAN ORIGINAL, WHICH INSPIRED THE CLASSIC BREAKFAST DISH KNOWN AS KEDGEREE. MADE WITH BASMATI RICE AND SMALL, TASTY LENTILS, THIS WILL MAKE AN AMPLE SUPPER OR BRUNCH DISH.

SERVES FOUR

INGREDIENTS

115g/4oz/1 cup Indian masoor
   dhal or Continental green lentils
1 onion, chopped
1 garlic clove, crushed
50g/2oz/4 tbsp vegetarian ghee or
   butter
30ml/2 tbsp sunflower oil
225g/8oz/1¼ cups easy-cook basmati
   rice
10ml/2 tsp ground coriander
10ml/2 tsp cumin seeds
2 cloves
3 cardamom pods
2 bay leaves
1 stick cinnamon
1 litre/1¾ pints/4 cups stock
30ml/2 tbsp tomato purée
salt and ground black pepper
45ml/3 tbsp fresh coriander or parsley,
   chopped, to garnish

1 Cover the dhal or lentils with boiling water and soak for 30 minutes. Drain and boil in fresh water for 10 minutes. Drain once more and set aside.

2 Fry the onion and garlic in the ghee or butter and oil in a large saucepan for about 5 minutes.

3 Add the rice, stir well to coat the grains in the ghee or butter and oil, then stir in the spices. Cook gently for a minute or so.

4 Add the lentils, stock, tomato purée and seasoning. Bring to the boil, then cover and simmer for 20 minutes until the stock is absorbed and the lentils and rice are just soft. Stir in the coriander or parsley and check the seasoning. Remove the cinnamon stick and bay leaf.

LEEKS IN EGG AND LEMON SAUCE

THE COMBINATION OF EGGS AND LEMON IN SAUCES AND SOUPS IS COMMONLY FOUND IN RECIPES FROM GREECE, TURKEY AND THE MIDDLE EAST. THIS SAUCE HAS A DELICIOUS FRESH TASTE AND BRINGS OUT THE BEST IN THE LEEKS. BE SURE TO USE TENDER BABY LEEKS FOR THIS RECIPE.

SERVES FOUR

INGREDIENTS

  675g/1½lb baby leeks
  15ml/1 tbsp cornflour
  10ml/2 tsp sugar
  2 egg yolks
  juice of 1½ lemons
  salt

1 Trim the leeks, slit them from top to bottom and rinse very well under cold water to remove any dirt.

2 Place the leeks in a large saucepan, preferably so they lie flat on the base, cover with water and add a little salt. Bring to the boil, cover and simmer for 4–5 minutes until just tender.

3 Carefully remove the leeks using a slotted spoon, drain well and arrange in a shallow serving dish. Reserve 200ml/7fl oz/scant 1 cup of the cooking liquid.

4 Blend the cornflour with the cooled cooking liquid and place in a small saucepan. Bring to the boil, stirring all the time, and cook over a gentle heat until the sauce thickens slightly. Stir in the sugar and then remove the saucepan from the heat and allow to cool slightly.

5 Beat the egg yolks thoroughly with the lemon juice and stir gradually into the cooled sauce. Cook over a very low heat, stirring all the time, until the sauce is fairly thick. Be careful not to overheat the sauce or it may curdle. As soon as the sauce has thickened remove the pan from the heat and continue stirring for a minute. Taste and add salt or sugar as necessary. Cool slightly.

6 Stir the cooled sauce with a wooden spoon. Pour the sauce over the leeks and then cover and chill well for at least 2 hours before serving.

PEANUT BUTTER FINGERS

CHILDREN LOVE THESE CRISPY CROQUETTES. FREEZE SOME READY TO FILL YOUNG TUMMIES!

MAKES 12

INGREDIENTS
1kg/2lb potatoes
1 large onion, chopped
2 large peppers, red or green, chopped
3 carrots, coarsely grated
45ml/3 tbsp sunflower oil
2 courgettes, coarsely grated
125g/4oz mushrooms, chopped
15ml/1 tbsp dried mixed herbs
115g/4oz Cheddar cheese, grated
75g/3oz/½ cup crunchy peanut butter
salt and ground black pepper
2 eggs, beaten
50g/2oz/½ cup dried breadcrumbs
45ml/3 tbsp dried Parmesan cheese
oil, for deep fat frying

1 Boil the potatoes until tender, then drain well and mash. Set aside.

2 Fry the onion, pepper and carrot in the oil for about 5 minutes, add the courgettes and mushrooms and cook for 5 minutes.

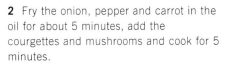

3 Mix the potato with the dried mixed herbs, grated cheese and peanut butter. Season, allow to cool for 30 minutes then stir in one of the eggs.

4 Spread out on a large plate, cool and chill, then divide into 12 portions and shape. Dip your hands in cold water if the mixture sticks.

5 Put the second egg in a bowl and dip the potato fingers into the egg first, then into the crumbs and Parmesan cheese until coated evenly. Put in fridge to set.

6 Heat oil in a deep fat frier to 190°C/375°F then fry the fingers in batches for about 3 minutes until golden. Drain well on kitchen paper towel. Serve hot.

COOK'S TIP
To reheat, thaw for about 1 hour, then grill or oven bake at 190°C/375°F/Gas 5 for 15 minutes.

YAM FRITTERS

YAMS HAVE A SLIGHTLY DRIER FLAVOUR THAN POTATOES AND ARE PARTICULARLY GOOD WHEN MIXED WITH SPICES AND THEN FRIED. THE FRITTERS CAN ALSO BE MOULDED INTO SMALL BALLS AND DEEP FRIED. THIS IS A FAVOURITE AFRICAN WAY OF SERVING YAMS.

MAKES ABOUT 18–20

INGREDIENTS
675g/1½lb yams
milk, for mashing
2 small eggs, beaten
45ml/3 tbsp chopped tomato flesh
45ml/3 tbsp finely chopped spring
  onions
1 green chilli, seeded and finely
  sliced
flour, for shaping
40g/1½oz white breadcrumbs
vegetable oil, for shallow frying
salt and freshly ground black pepper

1 Peel the yams and cut into chunks. Place in a saucepan of salted water and boil for 20–30 minutes until tender. Drain and mash with a little milk and about 45ml/3 tbsp of the beaten eggs.

2 Add the chopped tomato, spring onions, chilli and seasoning and stir well to mix thoroughly.

3 Using floured hands, shape the yam and vegetable mixture into round fritters, about 7.5cm/3in in diameter.

4 Dip each in the remaining beaten egg and then coat evenly with the breadcrumbs. Heat a little oil in a large frying pan and fry the yam fritters for about 4–5 minutes until golden brown. Turn the fritters over once during cooking. Drain well on kitchen paper and serve.

EDDO, CARROT <u>AND</u> PARSNIP MEDLEY

EDDO (TARO), LIKE YAMS, IS WIDELY EATEN IN AFRICA AND THE CARIBBEAN, OFTEN AS A PURÉE. HERE, IT IS ROASTED AND COMBINED WITH MORE COMMON ROOT VEGETABLES TO MAKE A COLOURFUL DISPLAY.

SERVES FOUR TO SIX

INGREDIENTS
450g/1lb eddoes (taros)
350g/12oz parsnips
450g/1lb carrots
25g/1oz butter
45ml/3 tbsp sunflower oil
For the dressing
30ml/2 tbsp fresh orange juice
30ml/2 tbsp demerara sugar
10ml/2 tsp soft green peppercorns
salt
fresh parsley, to garnish

1 Preheat the oven to 200°C/400°F/ Gas 6. Thickly peel the eddoes, making sure to remove all the skin as this can be an irritant. Cut into pieces about 5 x 2cm/2 x ¾in by 2cm/¾in, and place in a large bowl.

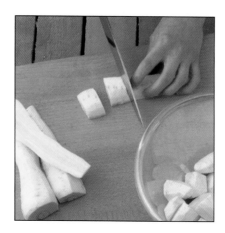

2 Peel the parsnips, halve lengthways and remove the inner core if necessary. Cut into the same size pieces as the eddo and add to the bowl. Blanch in boiling water for 2 minutes and then drain. Peel or scrub the carrots, and halve or quarter them according to their size.

3 Place the butter and sunflower oil in a roasting tin and heat in the oven for 3–4 minutes. Add the vegetables, turning them in the oil to coat evenly. Roast in the oven for 30 minutes.

4 Meanwhile, blend the orange juice, sugar and soft green peppercorns in a small bowl. Remove the roasting tin from the oven and allow to cool for a minute or so and then carefully pour the mixture over the vegetables, stirring to coat them all. (If the liquid is poured on immediately, the hot oil will spit.)

5 Return the tin to the oven and cook for a further 20 minutes until the vegetables are crisp and golden. Transfer to a warmed serving plate and sprinkle with salt. Garnish with parsley to serve.

ITALIAN ROAST PEPPERS

SIMPLE AND EFFECTIVE, THIS DISH WILL DELIGHT ANYONE WHO LIKES PEPPERS. IT CAN BE EATEN EITHER AS A STARTER SERVED WITH FRENCH BREAD, OR AS A LIGHT LUNCH WITH COUSCOUS OR RICE.

SERVES FOUR

INGREDIENTS

   4 small red peppers, halved, cored
     and seeded
   30–45ml/2–3 tbsp capers, chopped
   10–12 black olives, pitted
     and chopped
   2 garlic cloves, finely chopped
   50–75g/2–3 oz mozzarella, grated
   25–40g/1–1½oz fresh white
     breadcrumbs
   120ml/4fl oz/½ cup white wine
   45ml/3 tbsp olive oil
   5ml/1 tsp finely chopped fresh mint
   5ml/1 tsp chopped fresh parsley
   freshly ground black pepper

1 Preheat the oven to 180°C/350°F/ Gas 4 and butter a shallow ovenproof dish. Place the peppers tightly together in the dish and sprinkle over the chopped capers, black olives, garlic, mozzarella and breadcrumbs.

2 Pour over the wine and olive oil and then sprinkle with the mint, parsley and freshly ground black pepper.

3 Bake for 30–40 minutes until the topping is crisp and golden brown.

MARROWS WITH GNOCCHI

A SIMPLE WAY WITH MARROW, THIS DISH MAKES AN EXCELLENT ACCOMPANIMENT TO GRILLED MEAT BUT IT IS ALSO GOOD WITH A VEGETARIAN DISH, OR SIMPLY SERVED WITH GRILLED TOMATOES. GNOCCHI ARE AVAILABLE FROM MOST SUPERMARKETS; ITALIAN DELICATESSENS MAY ALSO SELL FRESH GNOCCHI.

SERVES FOUR

INGREDIENTS
1 small marrow, cut into
  bite-size chunks
50g/2oz butter
400g/14oz packet gnocchi
½ garlic clove, crushed
salt and freshly ground black pepper
chopped fresh basil, to garnish

1 Preheat the oven to 180°C/350°F/ Gas 4 and butter a large ovenproof dish. Place the marrow, more or less in a single layer, in the dish. Dot all over with the remaining butter.

2 Place a double piece of buttered greaseproof paper over the top. Cover with an ovenproof plate or lid so that it presses the marrow down, and then place a heavy, ovenproof weight on top of that. (Use a couple of old-fashioned scale weights.)

3 Put in the oven to bake for about 15 minutes, by which time the marrow should just be tender.

4 Cook the gnocchi in a large saucepan of boiling salted water for 2–3 minutes, or according to the instructions on the packet. Drain well.

5 Stir the garlic and gnocchi into the marrow. Season and then place the greaseproof paper over the marrow and return to the oven for 5 minutes (the weights are not necessary).

6 Just before serving, sprinkle the top with a little chopped fresh basil.

DINNERS

~

CELERIAC AND BLUE CHEESE ROULADE

CELERIAC ADDS A DELICATE AND SUBTLE FLAVOUR TO THIS ATTRACTIVE DISH. THE SPINACH ROULADE MAKES AN ATTRACTIVE CONTRAST TO THE CREAMY FILLING BUT YOU COULD USE A PLAIN OR CHEESE ROULADE BASE INSTEAD. BE SURE TO ROLL UP THE ROULADE WHILE IT IS STILL WARM AND PLIABLE.

SERVES SIX

INGREDIENTS
    15g/½oz butter
    225g/8oz cooked spinach, drained
      and chopped
    150ml/¼ pint/⅔ cup single cream
    4 large eggs, separated
    15g/½oz Parmesan cheese, grated
    pinch of nutmeg
    salt and freshly ground black pepper
For the filling
    225g/8oz celeriac
    lemon juice
    75g/3oz St Agur cheese
    115g/4oz fromage frais
    freshly ground black pepper

1 Preheat the oven to 200°C/400°F/
Gas 6 and line a 34 x 24cm/13 x 9in Swiss
roll tin with non-stick baking paper.

2 Melt the butter in a saucepan and add
the spinach. Cook gently until all the
liquid has evaporated, stirring frequently.
Remove the pan from the heat and stir in
the cream, egg yolks, Parmesan cheese,
nutmeg and seasoning.

3 Whisk the egg whites until stiff, fold
them gently into the spinach mixture and
then spoon into the prepared tin. Spread
the mixture evenly and use a palette
knife to smooth the surface.

4 Bake in the oven for 10–15 minutes
until the roulade is firm to the touch and
lightly golden on top. Carefully turn out
on to a sheet of greaseproof or non-stick
baking paper and peel away the lining
paper. Roll it up with the paper inside
and leave to cool slightly.

5 To make the filling, peel and grate the
celeriac into a bowl and sprinkle well
with lemon juice. Blend the blue cheese
and fromage frais together and mix with
the celeriac and a little black pepper.

6 Unroll the roulade, spread with the
filling and roll up again. Serve at once or
wrap loosely and chill.

LOOFAH AND AUBERGINE RATATOUILLE

LOOFAHS HAVE A SIMILAR FLAVOUR TO COURGETTES AND CONSEQUENTLY TASTE EXCELLENT WITH AUBERGINES AND TOMATOES. BE SURE TO USE VERY YOUNG LOOFAHS AND ALSO ENSURE THAT YOU PEEL AWAY THE ROUGH SKIN, AS IT CAN BE SHARP.

SERVES FOUR

INGREDIENTS
  1 large or 2 medium aubergines
  450g/1lb young loofahs or
    sponge gourds
  1 large red pepper, cut into
    large chunks
  225g/8oz cherry tomatoes
  225g/8oz shallots, peeled
  10ml/2 tsp ground coriander
  60ml/4 tbsp olive oil
  2 garlic cloves, finely chopped
  a few coriander leaves
  salt and freshly ground black pepper

1 Cut the aubergine into thick chunks and sprinkle the pieces with salt. Set aside in a colander for about 45 minutes and then rinse well under cold running water and pat dry.

2 Preheat the oven to 220°C/425°F/ Gas 7. Peel and slice the loofahs into 2cm/¾in pieces. Place the aubergine, loofah and pepper pieces, together with the tomatoes and shallots in a roasting pan which is large enough to take all the vegetables in a single layer.

3 Sprinkle with the ground coriander and olive oil and then scatter the chopped garlic and coriander leaves on top. Season to taste.

4 Roast for about 25 minutes, stirring the vegetables occasionally, until the loofah is golden brown and the peppers are beginning to char at the edges.

RADICCHIO PIZZA

THIS UNUSUAL PIZZA TOPPING CONSISTS OF CHOPPED RADICCHIO WITH LEEKS, TOMATOES AND PARMESAN AND MOZZARELLA CHEESES. THE BASE IS A SCONE DOUGH, MAKING THIS A QUICK AND EASY SUPPER DISH TO PREPARE. SERVE WITH A CRISP GREEN SALAD.

SERVES TWO

INGREDIENTS

½ x 400g/14oz can chopped tomatoes
2 garlic cloves, crushed
pinch of dried basil
25ml/1½ tbsp olive oil, plus extra
  for dipping
2 leeks, sliced
100g/3½oz radicchio, roughly
  chopped
20g/¾oz Parmesan, grated
115g/4oz mozzarella cheese, sliced
10–12 black olives, pitted
basil leaves, to garnish
salt and freshly ground black pepper
For the dough
225g/8oz self-raising flour
2.5ml/½ tsp salt
50g/2oz butter or margarine
about 120ml/4fl oz/½ cup milk

1 Preheat the oven to 220°C/425°F/
Gas 7 and grease a baking sheet. Mix the flour and salt in a bowl, rub in the butter or margarine and gradually stir in the milk and mix to a soft dough.

2 Roll the dough out on a lightly floured surface to make a 25–28cm/10–11in round. Place on the baking sheet.

3 Purée the tomatoes and then pour into a small saucepan. Stir in one of the crushed garlic cloves, together with the dried basil and seasoning, and simmer over a moderate heat until the mixture is thick and reduced by about half.

4 Heat the olive oil in a large frying pan and fry the leeks and remaining garlic for 4–5 minutes until slightly softened. Add the radicchio and cook, stirring continuously for a few minutes, and then cover and simmer gently for about 5–10 minutes. Stir in the Parmesan cheese and season with salt and pepper.

5 Cover the dough base with the tomato mixture and then spoon the leek and radicchio mixture on top. Arrange the mozzarella slices on top and scatter over the black olives. Dip a few basil leaves in olive oil, arrange on top and then bake the pizza for 15–20 minutes until the scone base and top are golden brown.

TAGLIATELLE FUNGI

THE MUSHROOM SAUCE IS QUICK TO MAKE AND THE PASTA COOKS VERY QUICKLY; BOTH NEED TO BE COOKED AS NEAR TO SERVING AS POSSIBLE SO CAREFUL COORDINATION IS REQUIRED. PUT THE PASTA IN TO COOK WHEN THE MASCARPONE CHEESE IS ADDED TO THE SAUCE.

SERVES FOUR

INGREDIENTS
    about 50g/2oz butter
    225–350g/8–12oz chanterelles
        or other wild mushrooms
    15ml/1 tbsp plain flour
    150ml/¼ pint/⅔ cup milk
    90ml/6 tbsp crème fraîche
    15ml/1 tbsp chopped fresh parsley
    275g/10oz fresh tagliatelle
    olive oil
    salt and freshly ground black
        pepper

1 Melt 40g/1½oz of the butter in a frying pan and fry the mushrooms for about 2–3 minutes over a gentle heat until the juices begin to run, then increase the heat and cook until the liquid has almost evaporated. Transfer the mushrooms to a bowl using a slotted spoon.

2 Stir in the flour, adding a little more butter if necessary, and cook for about 1 minute, and then gradually stir in the milk to make a smooth sauce.

3 Add the crème fraîche, parsley, mushrooms and seasoning and stir well. Cook very gently to heat through and then keep warm while cooking the pasta.

4 Cook the pasta in a large saucepan of boiling water for 4–5 minutes (or according to the instructions on the packet). Drain well, toss in a little olive oil and then turn on to a warmed serving plate. Pour the mushroom sauce over and serve immediately.

COOK'S TIP
Chanterelles are a little tricky to wash, as they are so delicate. However, since these are woodland mushrooms, it's important to clean them thoroughly. Hold each one by the stalk and let cold water run under the gills to dislodge hidden dirt. Shake gently to dry.

TANGY FRICASSEE

*VEGETABLES IN A LIGHT TANGY
SAUCE AND COVERED WITH A
CRISPY CRUMB TOPPING MAKE A
SIMPLE AND EASY MAIN COURSE
TO SERVE WITH CRUSTY BREAD
AND SALAD.*

SERVES FOUR

INGREDIENTS
  4 courgettes, sliced
  115g/4oz green beans, sliced
  4 large tomatoes, skinned and sliced
  1 onion, sliced
  50g/2oz/4 tbsp butter or sunflower
    margarine
  40g/1½oz/⅓ cup plain flour
  10ml/2 tsp coarse grain mustard
  450ml/¾ pint/2 cups milk
  150ml/¼ pint/⅔ cup natural yogurt
  5ml/1 tsp dried thyme
  115g/4oz mature cheese, grated
  salt and ground black pepper
  60ml/4 tbsp fresh wholemeal
    breadcrumbs tossed with 15ml/1 tbsp
    sunflower oil

1 Blanch the courgettes and beans in a small amount of boiling water for just 5 minutes, then drain and arrange in a shallow ovenproof dish. Arrange all but three slices of tomato on top. Put the onion into a saucepan with the butter or margarine and fry gently for 5 minutes.

2 Stir in the flour and mustard, cook for a minute then add the milk gradually until the sauce has thickened. Simmer for a further 2 minutes.

3 Remove the pan from the heat, add the yogurt, thyme and cheese, stirring until melted. Season to taste. Reheat gently if you wish, but do not allow the sauce to boil or it will curdle.

4 Pour the sauce over the vegetables and scatter the breadcrumbs on top. Brown under a preheated grill until golden and crisp, taking care not to let them burn. Garnish with the reserved tomato slices if desired.

WILD MUSHROOMS IN BRIOCHE

SERVES FOUR

INGREDIENTS
    4 small brioches
    olive oil, for glazing
    20ml/4 tsp lemon juice
    sprigs of parsley, to garnish
For the mushroom filling
    25g/1oz butter
    2 shallots
    1 garlic clove, crushed
    175–225g/6–8oz assorted wild
      mushrooms, halved if large
    45ml/3 tbsp white wine
    45ml/3 tbsp double cream
    5ml/1 tsp chopped fresh basil
    5ml/1 tsp chopped fresh parsley
    salt and freshly ground black pepper

1 Preheat the oven to 180°C/350°F/
Gas 4. Using a serrated or grapefruit
knife, cut a circle out of the top of each
brioche and reserve. Scoop out the
bread inside to make a small cavity.

2 Place the brioches and the tops on a
baking sheet and brush inside and out
with olive oil. Bake for 7–10 minutes
until golden and crisp. Squeeze 5ml/
1 tsp of lemon juice inside each brioche.

3 To make the filling, melt the butter in
a frying pan and fry the shallots and
garlic for 2–3 minutes until softened.

4 Add the mushrooms and cook gently
for about 4–5 minutes, stirring.

5 When the juices begin to run, reduce
the heat and continue cooking for about
3–4 minutes, stirring occasionally, until
the pan is fairly dry.

6 Stir in the wine. Cook for a few more
minutes and then stir in the cream, basil,
parsley and seasoning to taste.

7 Pile the mushroom mixture into the
brioche shells and return to the oven and
reheat for about 5–6 minutes. Serve as a
starter, garnished with a sprig of parsley.

WILD MUSHROOMS WITH PANCAKES

SERVES SIX

INGREDIENTS
    225–275g/8–10oz assorted wild
      mushrooms
    50g/2oz butter
    1–2 garlic cloves
    splash of brandy (optional)
    freshly ground black pepper
    soured cream, to serve
For the pancakes
    115g/4oz self-raising flour
    20g/¾oz buckwheat flour
    2.5ml/½ tsp baking powder
    2 eggs
    about 250ml/8fl oz/1 cup milk
    pinch of salt
    oil, for frying

1 To make the pancakes, mix together
the flours, baking powder and salt in a
large bowl or food processor. Add the
eggs and milk and beat or process to
make a smooth batter, about the
consistency of single cream.

2 Grease a large griddle or frying pan
with a little oil and when hot, pour small
amounts of batter (about 15–30ml/
1–2 tbsp per pancake) on to the griddle,
well spaced apart.

3 Fry for a few minutes until bubbles
begin to appear on the surface and the
underside is golden, and then flip over.
Cook for about 1 minute until golden.
Keep warm, wrapped in a clean dish
towel. (Makes about 18–20 pancakes.)

4 If the mushrooms are large, cut them
in half. Melt the butter in a frying pan
and add the garlic and mushrooms. Fry
over a moderate heat for a few minutes
until the juices begin to run and then
increase the heat and cook, stirring
frequently, until nearly all the juices have
evaporated. Stir in the brandy, if using,
and season with a little black pepper.

5 Arrange the warm pancakes on a
serving plate and spoon over a little
soured cream. Top with the hot
mushrooms and serve immediately.

COOK'S TIP
This makes a delicious and elegant
starter for a dinner party. Alternatively,
make cocktail-size pancakes and serve
as part of a buffet supper.

KOHLRABI STUFFED WITH PEPPERS

IF YOU HAVEN'T SAMPLED KOHLRABI, OR HAVE ONLY EATEN IT IN STEWS WHERE ITS FLAVOUR IS LOST, THIS DISH IS RECOMMENDED. THE SLIGHTLY SHARP FLAVOUR OF THE PEPPERS IS AN EXCELLENT FOIL TO THE MORE EARTHY FLAVOUR OF THE KOHLRABI.

SERVES FOUR

INGREDIENTS

    4 small kohlrabi, about 175–225g/
      6–8oz each
    about 400ml/14fl oz/1⅔ cups hot
      vegetable stock
    15ml/1 tbsp olive or sunflower oil
    1 onion, chopped
    1 small red pepper, seeded and sliced
    1 small green pepper, seeded
      and sliced
    salt and freshly ground black pepper
    flat leaf parsley, to garnish (optional)

1 Preheat the oven to 180°C/350°F/ Gas 4. Trim and top and tail the kohlrabi and arrange in the base of a medium-size ovenproof dish.

2 Pour over the stock to come about halfway up the vegetables. Cover and braise in the oven for about 30 minutes until tender. Transfer to a plate and allow to cool, reserving the stock.

3 Heat the oil in a frying pan and fry the onion for 3–4 minutes over a gentle heat, stirring occasionally. Add the peppers and cook for a further 2–3 minutes, until the onion is lightly browned.

4 Add the reserved vegetable stock and a little seasoning, then simmer, uncovered, over a moderate heat until the stock has almost evaporated.

5 Scoop out the flesh from the kohlrabi and roughly chop. Stir the flesh into the onion and pepper mixture, taste and adjust the seasoning. Arrange the shells in a shallow ovenproof dish.

6 Spoon the filling into the kohlrabi shells. Place in the oven for 5–10 minutes to heat through and then serve, garnished with flat leaf parsley, if liked.

LEEK SOUFFLÉ

SOME PEOPLE THINK OF A SOUFFLÉ AS A DINNER PARTY DISH, AND A RATHER TRICKY ONE AT THAT. HOWEVER, OTHERS FREQUENTLY SERVE THEM FOR FAMILY MEALS BECAUSE THEY ARE QUICK AND EASY TO MAKE, AND PROVE TO BE VERY POPULAR AND SATISFYING.

SERVES TWO TO THREE

INGREDIENTS
    15ml/1 tbsp sunflower oil
    40g/1½oz butter
    2 leeks, thinly sliced
    about 300ml/½ pint/1¼ cups milk
    25g/1oz plain flour
    4 eggs, separated
    75g/3oz Gruyère or Emmenthal
        cheese, grated
    salt and freshly ground black pepper

1 Preheat the oven to 180°C/350°F Gas 4 and butter a large soufflé dish. Heat the oil and 15g/½oz of the butter in a small saucepan or flameproof casserole and fry the leeks over a gentle heat for 4–5 minutes until soft but not brown, stirring occasionally.

2 Stir in the milk and bring to the boil. Cover and simmer for 4–5 minutes until the leeks are tender. Strain the liquid through a sieve into a measuring jug.

3 Melt the remaining butter in a saucepan, stir in the flour and cook for 1 minute. Remove pan from the heat. Make up the reserved liquid with milk to 300ml/ ½ pint/1¼ cups. Gradually stir the milk into the pan to make a smooth sauce. Return to the heat and bring to the boil, stirring. When thickened, remove from the heat. Cool slightly and then beat in the egg yolks, cheese and the leeks.

4 Whisk the egg whites until stiff and, using a large metal spoon, fold into the leek and egg mixture. Pour into the prepared soufflé dish and bake in the oven for about 30 minutes until golden and puffy. Serve immediately.

SPINACH RAVIOLI

HOME-MADE RAVIOLI IS TIME-CONSUMING, YET IT IS WORTH THE EFFORT AS EVEN THE BEST SHOP-BOUGHT PASTA NEVER TASTES QUITE AS FRESH. TO COMPLEMENT THIS EFFORT, MAKE THE FILLING EXACTLY TO YOUR LIKING, TASTING IT FOR THE RIGHT BALANCE OF SPINACH AND CHEESE.

SERVES FOUR

INGREDIENTS
225g/8oz fresh spinach
40g/1½oz butter
1 small onion, finely chopped
25g/1oz Parmesan cheese, grated
40g/1½oz dolcellate cheese,
   crumbled
15ml/1 tbsp chopped fresh parsley
salt and freshly ground black pepper
shavings of Parmesan cheese, to serve
For the pasta dough
350g/12oz strong white flour
4ml/¾ tsp salt
2 eggs
15ml/1 tbsp olive oil

1 To make the pasta dough, mix together the flour and salt in a large bowl or food processor. Add the eggs, olive oil and about 45ml/3 tbsp of cold water or enough to make a pliable dough. If working by hand, mix the ingredients together and then knead the dough for about 15 minutes until very smooth. Or, process for about 1½ minutes in a food processor. Place the dough in a plastic bag and chill for at least 1 hour (or overnight if more convenient).

2 Cook the spinach in a large, covered saucepan for 3–4 minutes, until the leaves have wilted. Strain and press out the excess liquid. Set aside to cool a little and then chop finely.

3 Melt half the butter in a small saucepan and fry the onion over a gentle heat for about 5–6 minutes until soft. Place in a bowl with the chopped spinach, the Parmesan and dolcellate cheeses, and seasoning. Mix well.

4 Grease a ravioli tin. Roll out half or a quarter of the pasta dough to a thickness of about 3mm/⅛in. Lay the dough over the ravioli tin, pressing it well into each of the squares.

5 Spoon a little spinach mixture into each cavity, then roll out a second piece of dough and lay it on top. Press a rolling pin evenly over the top of the tin to seal the edges and then cut the ravioli into squares using a pastry cutter.

6 Place the ravioli in a large saucepan of boiling water and simmer for about 4–5 minutes until cooked through but *al dente*. Drain well and then toss with the remaining butter and the parsley.

7 Divide between four serving plates and serve scattered with shavings of Parmesan cheese.

COOK'S TIP
For a small ravioli tin of 32 holes, divide the dough into quarters. Roll the dough out until it covers the tin comfortably – it takes some time but the pasta needs to be thin otherwise the ravioli will be too stodgy. For a large ravioli tin of 64 holes, divide the dough in half.

SPINACH AND CANNELLINI BEANS

THIS HEARTY DISH CAN BE MADE WITH ALMOST ANY DRIED BEAN, SUCH AS BLACK-EYED BEANS, HARICOTS OR CHICK-PEAS. IT IS A GOOD DISH TO SERVE ON A COLD EVENING. IF USING CANNED BEANS, DRAIN, THEN RINSE UNDER COLD WATER.

SERVES FOUR

INGREDIENTS
225g/8oz cannellini beans,
  soaked overnight
60ml/4 tbsp olive oil
1 slice white bread
1 onion, chopped
3–4 tomatoes, peeled and chopped
a good pinch of paprika
450g/1lb spinach
1 garlic clove, halved
salt and freshly ground black pepper

1 Drain the beans, place in a saucepan and cover with water. Bring to the boil and boil rapidly for 10 minutes. Cover and simmer for about 1 hour until the beans are tender. Drain.

2 Heat 30ml/2 tbsp of the oil in a frying pan and fry the bread until golden brown. Transfer to a plate.

3 Fry the onion in 15ml/1 tbsp of the oil over a gentle heat until soft but not brown, then add the tomatoes and continue cooking over a gentle heat.

4 Heat the remaining oil in a large pan, stir in the paprika and then add the spinach. Cover and cook for a few minutes until the spinach has wilted.

5 Add the onion and tomato mixture to the spinach, mix well and stir in the cannellini beans. Place the garlic and fried bread in a food processor and process until smooth. Stir into the spinach and bean mixture. Add 150ml/ ¼ pint/⅔ cup cold water and then cover and simmer gently for 20–30 minutes, adding more water if necessary.

SWEETCORN AND CHEESE PASTIES

THESE TASTY PASTIES ARE REALLY SIMPLE TO MAKE AND EXTREMELY MOREISH — WHY NOT MAKE DOUBLE THE AMOUNT — THEY'LL GO LIKE HOT CAKES.

MAKES EIGHTEEN TO TWENTY

INGREDIENTS
    250g/9oz sweetcorn
    115g/4oz feta cheese
    1 egg, beaten
    30ml/2 tbsp whipping cream
    15g/½oz Parmesan cheese, grated
    3 spring onions, chopped
    8–10 small sheets filo pastry
    115g/4oz butter, melted
    freshly ground black pepper

1 Preheat the oven to 190°C/375°F/ Gas 5 and butter two patty tins.

2 If using fresh sweetcorn, strip the kernels from the cob using a sharp knife and simmer in a little salted water for 3–5 minutes until tender. For canned sweetcorn, drain and rinse well under cold running water.

3 Crumble the feta cheese into a bowl and stir in the sweetcorn. Add the egg, cream, Parmesan cheese, spring onions and ground black pepper, and stir well.

4 Take one sheet of pastry and cut it in half to make a square. (Keep the remaining pastry covered with a damp cloth to prevent it drying out.) Brush with melted butter and then fold into four, to make a smaller square (about 7.5cm/3in).

5 Place a heaped teaspoon of mixture in the centre of each pastry square and then squeeze the pastry around the filling to make a "money bag" casing.

6 Continue making pasties until all the mixture is used up. Brush the outside of each "bag" with any remaining butter and then bake in the oven for about 15 minutes until golden. Serve hot.

CASSAVA AND VEGETABLE KEBABS

THIS IS AN ATTRACTIVE AND DELICIOUS ASSORTMENT OF AFRICAN VEGETABLES, MARINATED IN A SPICY GARLIC SAUCE. IF CASSAVA IS UNAVAILABLE, USE SWEET POTATO OR YAM INSTEAD.

SERVES FOUR

INGREDIENTS
175g/6oz cassava
1 onion, cut into wedges
1 aubergine, cut into bite-size pieces
1 courgette, sliced
1 ripe plantain, sliced
1 red pepper or ½ red pepper, ½ green pepper, sliced
16 cherry tomatoes
For the marinade
60ml/4 tbsp lemon juice
60ml/4 tbsp olive oil
45–60/3–4 tbsp soy sauce
15ml/1 tbsp tomato purée
1 green chilli, seeded and finely chopped
½ onion, grated
2 garlic cloves, crushed
5ml/1 tsp mixed spice
pinch of dried thyme
rice or couscous, to serve

1 Peel the cassava and cut into bite-size pieces. Place in a bowl, cover with boiling water and leave to blanch for 5 minutes. Drain well.

2 Place all the vegetables, including the cassava, in a large bowl.

3 Blend together all the marinade ingredients and pour over the prepared vegetables. Set aside for 1–2 hours.

4 Preheat the grill and thread all the vegetables and cherry tomatoes on to eight skewers.

5 Grill the vegetables under a low heat for about 15 minutes until tender and browned, turning frequently and basting occasionally with the marinade.

6 Meanwhile, pour the remaining marinade into a small saucepan and simmer for 10 minutes until slightly reduced.

7 Arrange the vegetable kebabs on a serving plate and strain the sauce into a small jug. Serve with rice or couscous.

TURNIP AND CHICK-PEA COBBLER

A GOOD MID-WEEK MEAL.

SERVES FOUR TO SIX

INGREDIENTS

 1 onion, sliced
 2 carrots, chopped
 3 medium size turnips, chopped
 1 small sweet potato or swede, chopped
 2 celery sticks, sliced thinly
 45ml/3 tbsp sunflower oil
 2.5ml/½ tsp ground coriander
 2.5ml/½ tsp dried mixed herbs
 1 × 425g/15oz can chopped tomatoes
 1 × 400g/14oz can chick-peas
 1 vegetable stock cube
 salt and ground black pepper
For the topping
 225g/8oz/2 cups self-raising flour
 5ml/1 tsp baking powder
 50g/2oz/4 tbsp margarine
 45ml/3 tbsp sunflower seeds
 30ml/2 tbsp Parmesan cheese, grated
 150ml/¼ pint/⅔ cup milk

1 Fry all the vegetables in the oil for about 10 minutes until they are soft. Add the coriander, herbs, tomatoes, chick peas with their liquor and stock cube. Season well and simmer for 20 minutes.

2 Pour the vegetables into a shallow casserole dish while you make the topping. Preheat the oven to 190°C/375°F/Gas 5.

3 Mix together the flour and baking powder then rub in the margarine until it resembles fine crumbs. Stir in the seeds and Parmesan cheese. Add the milk and mix to a firm dough.

4 Lightly roll out the topping to a thickness of 1cm/½ in and stamp out star shapes or rounds, or simply cut it into small squares.

5 Place the shapes on top of the vegetable mixture and brush with a little extra milk. Bake for 12–15 minutes until risen and golden brown. Serve hot with green, leafy vegetables.

BAKED LEEKS WITH CHEESE AND YOGURT TOPPING

LIKE ALL VEGETABLES, THE FRESHER LEEKS ARE, THE BETTER THEIR FLAVOUR, AND THE FRESHEST LEEKS AVAILABLE SHOULD BE USED FOR THIS DISH. SMALL, YOUNG LEEKS ARE AROUND AT THE BEGINNING OF THE SEASON AND ARE PERFECT TO USE HERE.

SERVES FOUR

INGREDIENTS

    8 small leeks, about 675g/1½lb
    2 small eggs or 1 large one, beaten
    150g/5oz fresh goat's cheese
    85ml/3fl oz/⅓ cup natural yogurt
    50g/2oz Parmesan cheese, grated
    25g/1oz fresh white or brown
      breadcrumbs
    salt and freshly ground black pepper

1 Preheat the oven to 180°C/350°F/Gas 4 and butter a shallow ovenproof dish. Trim the leeks, cut a slit from top to bottom and rinse well under cold water.

2 Place the leeks in a saucepan of water, bring to the boil and simmer gently for 6–8 minutes until just tender. Remove and drain well using a slotted spoon, and arrange in the prepared dish.

3 Beat the eggs with the goat's cheese, yogurt and half the Parmesan cheese, and season well with salt and pepper.

4 Pour the cheese and yogurt mixture over the leeks. Mix the breadcrumbs and remaining Parmesan cheese together and sprinkle over the sauce. Bake in the oven for 35–40 minutes until the top is crisp and golden brown.

CAULIFLOWER AND MUSHROOM GOUGÈRE

THIS IS AN ALL-ROUND FAVOURITE VEGETARIAN DISH. WHEN COOKING THIS DISH FOR MEAT LOVERS,
CHOPPED ROAST HAM OR FRIED BACON CAN BE ADDED.

SERVES FOUR TO SIX

INGREDIENTS
    300ml/½ pint/1¼ cups water
    115g/4oz butter or margarine
    150g/5oz plain flour
    4 eggs
    115g/4oz Gruyère or Cheddar cheese,
      finely diced
    5ml/1 tsp Dijon mustard
    salt and freshly ground black pepper
For the filling
    ½ x 400g/14oz can tomatoes
    15ml/1 tbsp sunflower oil
    15g/½oz butter or margarine
    1 onion, chopped
    115g/4oz button mushrooms, halved
      if large
    1 small cauliflower, broken into
      small florets
    sprig of thyme
    salt and freshly ground black pepper

1 Preheat the oven to 200°C/400°F/
Gas 6 and butter a large ovenproof dish.
Place the water and butter together in a
large saucepan and heat until the butter
has melted. Remove from the heat and
add all the flour at once. Beat well with a
wooden spoon for about 30 seconds until
smooth. Allow to cool slightly.

2 Beat in the eggs, one at a time, and
continue beating until the mixture is
thick and glossy. Stir in the cheese and
mustard and season with salt and
pepper. Spread the mixture around the
sides of the ovenproof dish, leaving a
hollow in the centre for the filling.

3 To make the filling, purée the
tomatoes in a blender or food processor
and then pour into a measuring jug. Add
enough water to make up to 300ml/
½ pint/1¼ cups of liquid.

4 Heat the oil and butter in a flameproof
casserole and fry the onion for about
3–4 minutes until softened but not
browned. Add the mushrooms and cook
for 2–3 minutes until they begin to be
flecked with brown. Add the cauliflower
florets and stir-fry for 1 minute.

5 Add the tomato liquid, thyme and
seasoning. Cook, uncovered, over a
gentle heat for about 5 minutes until the
cauliflower is only just tender.

6 Spoon the mixture into the hollow in
the ovenproof dish, adding all the liquid.
Bake in the oven for about 35–40
minutes, until the outer pastry is well
risen and golden brown.

COOK'S TIP
For a variation, ham or bacon can be
added. Use about 115–150g/4–5oz
thickly sliced roast ham and add to the
sauce at the end of step 5.

SPINACH IN FILO WITH THREE CHEESES

A GOOD CHOICE TO SERVE WHEN VEGETARIANS AND MEAT EATERS ARE GATHERED FOR A MEAL AS, WHATEVER THEIR PREFERENCE, EVERYONE SEEMS PARTIAL TO THIS TASTY DISH.

SERVES FOUR

INGREDIENTS

450g/1lb spinach
15ml/1 tbsp sunflower oil
15g/½oz butter
1 small onion, finely chopped
175g/6oz ricotta cheese
115g/4oz feta cheese, cut into
  small cubes
75g/3oz Gruyère or Emmenthal
  cheese, grated
15ml/1 tbsp fresh chopped chervil
5ml/1 tsp fresh chopped marjoram
salt and freshly ground black pepper
5 large or 10 small sheets filo pastry
40–50g/1½–2oz butter, melted

1 Preheat the oven to 190°C/375°F/ Gas 5. Cook the spinach in a large saucepan over a moderate heat for 3–4 minutes until the leaves have wilted, shaking the saucepan occasionally. Strain and press out the excess liquid.

2 Heat the oil and butter in a saucepan and fry the onion for 3–4 minutes until softened. Remove from the heat and add half of the spinach. Combine, using a metal spoon to break up the spinach.

3 Add the ricotta cheese and stir until evenly combined. Stir in the remaining spinach, again chopping it into the mixture with a metal spoon. Fold in the feta and Gruyère or Emmenthal cheese, chervil, marjoram and seasoning.

4 Lay a sheet of filo pastry measuring about 30cm/12 in square on a work surface. (If you have small filo sheets, lay them side by side, overlapping by about 2.5cm/1in in the middle.) Brush with melted butter and cover with a second sheet; brush this with butter and build up five layers of pastry in this way.

5 Spread the filling over the pastry, leaving a 2.5cm/1in border. Fold the sides inwards and then roll up.

6 Place the roll, seam side down, on a greased baking sheet and brush with the remaining butter. Bake in the oven for about 30 minutes until golden brown.

Eggs Flamenco

A variation of the popular Basque dish Piperade, the eggs are cooked whole instead of beating them before adding to the pepper mixture. The recipe is known as Chakchouka in North Africa and makes a good lunch or supper dish.

SERVES FOUR

INGREDIENTS
    2 red peppers
    1 green pepper
    30ml/2 tbsp olive oil
    1 large onion, finely sliced
    2 garlic cloves, crushed
    5–6 tomatoes, peeled and chopped
    120ml/4fl oz/½ cup puréed canned
      tomatoes or tomato juice
    good pinch of dried basil
    4 eggs
    40ml/8 tsp single cream
    pinch of cayenne pepper (optional)
    salt and freshly ground black pepper

1 Preheat the oven to 180°C/350°F/ Gas 4. Seed and thinly slice the peppers. Heat the olive oil in a large frying pan. Fry the onion and garlic gently for about 5 minutes, stirring, until softened.

2 Add the peppers to the onion and fry for 10 minutes. Stir in the tomatoes and tomato purée or juice, the basil and seasoning. Cook gently for a further 10 minutes until the peppers are soft.

3 Spoon the mixture into four ovenproof dishes, preferably earthenware. Make a hole in the centre and break an egg into each. Spoon 10ml/2 tsp cream over the yolk of each egg and sprinkle with a little black pepper or cayenne, as preferred.

4 Bake in the oven for 12–15 minutes until the white of the egg is lightly set. Serve at once with chunks of crusty warm French or Spanish bread.

BAKED MARROW IN PARSLEY SAUCE

THIS IS A REALLY GLORIOUS WAY WITH A SIMPLE AND MODEST VEGETABLE. TRY TO FIND A SMALL, FIRM AND UNBLEMISHED MARROW FOR THIS RECIPE, AS THE FLAVOUR WILL BE SWEET, FRESH AND DELICATE. YOUNG MARROWS DO NOT NEED PEELING; MORE MATURE ONES DO.

SERVES FOUR

INGREDIENTS
    1 small young marrow, about 900g/2lb
    30ml/2 tbsp olive oil
    15g/½oz butter
    1 onion, chopped
    15ml/1 tbsp plain flour
    300ml/½ pint/1¼ cups milk
      and single cream mixed
    30ml/2 tbsp chopped fresh parsley
    salt and freshly ground black pepper

1 Preheat the oven to 180°C/350°F/
Gas 4 and cut the marrow into pieces
measuring about 5 x 2.5cm/2 x 1in.

2 Heat the oil and butter in a flameproof
casserole and fry the onion over a gentle
heat until very soft.

3 Add the marrow and sauté for
1–2 minutes and then stir in the flour.
Cook for a few minutes, then stir in the
milk and cream mixture.

4 Add the parsley and seasoning, stir
well and then cover and cook in the oven
for 30–35 minutes. If liked, remove the
lid for the final 5 minutes of cooking to
brown the top. Alternatively, serve the
marrow in its rich pale sauce.

COOK'S TIP
Chopped fresh basil or a mixture of basil
and chervil also tastes good in this dish.

FESTIVE JALOUSIE

An excellent pie to serve during the holiday period. Use Chinese dried chestnuts, soaked and cooked, instead of fresh ones.

SERVES SIX

INGREDIENTS

   450g/1lb puff pastry, thawed if frozen
   450g/1lb Brussels sprouts, trimmed
   16 whole chestnuts, peeled if fresh
   1 large red pepper, sliced
   1 large onion, sliced
   45ml/3 tbsp sunflower oil
   1 egg yolk, beaten with 15ml/1 tbsp
     water
For the sauce
   40g/1½oz/scant ½ cup plain flour
   40g/1½oz/3 tbsp butter
   300ml/½ pint milk
   75g/3oz Cheddar cheese, grated
   30ml/2 tbsp dry sherry
   good pinch dried sage
   salt and ground black pepper
   45ml/3 tbsp fresh parsley, chopped

2 Blanch the Brussels sprouts for 4 minutes in 300ml/½ pint/1¼ cups boiling water then drain, reserving the water. Refresh the sprouts under cold running water.

3 Cut each chestnut in half. Lightly fry the red pepper and onion in the oil for 5 minutes. Set aside till later.

6 Fit the larger piece of pastry into your pie dish and layer the sprouts, chestnuts, peppers and onions on top. Trickle over the sauce, making sure it seeps through to wet the vegetables.

7 Brush the pastry edges with beaten egg yolk and fit the second pastry sheet on top, pressing the edges well to seal them.

8 Crimp, knock up the edges then mark the centre. Glaze well all over with egg yolk. Set aside to rest somewhere cool while you preheat the oven to 200°C/400°F/Gas 6. Bake for 30–40 minutes until golden brown and crisp.

1 Roll out the pastry to make two large rectangles, roughly the size of your dish. The pastry should be about 6mm/¼in thick and one rectangle should be slightly larger than the other. Set the pastry aside in the refrigerator.

4 Make up the sauce by beating the flour, butter and milk together over a medium heat. Beat the sauce continuously, bringing it to the boil, stirring until it is thickened and smooth.

5 Stir in the reserved sprout water, and the cheese, sherry, sage and seasoning. Simmer for 3 minutes to reduce and mix in the parsley.

CELERIAC GRATIN

ALTHOUGH CELERIAC HAS A RATHER UNATTRACTIVE APPEARANCE WITH ITS HARD, KNOBBLY SKIN, IT IS A VEGETABLE THAT HAS A VERY DELICIOUS SWEET AND NUTTY FLAVOUR. THIS IS ACCENTUATED IN THIS DISH BY THE ADDITION OF THE SWEET YET NUTTY EMMENTAL CHEESE.

SERVES FOUR

INGREDIENTS
450g/1lb celeriac
juice of ½ lemon
25g/1oz butter
1 small onion, finely chopped
30ml/2 tbsp plain flour
300ml/½ pint/1¼ cups milk
25g/1oz Emmental cheese, grated
15ml/1 tbsp capers
salt and cayenne pepper

1 Preheat the oven to 190°C/375°F/ Gas 5. Peel the celeriac and cut into 5mm/¼in slices, immediately plunging them into a saucepan of cold water acidulated with the lemon juice.

2 Bring the water to the boil and simmer the celeriac for 10–12 minutes until just tender. Drain and arrange the celeriac in a shallow ovenproof dish.

3 Melt the butter in a small saucepan and fry the onion over a gentle heat until soft but not browned. Stir in the flour, cook for 1 minute and then slowly stir in the milk to make a smooth sauce. Stir in the cheese, capers and seasoning to taste and then pour over the celeriac. Cook in the oven for 15–20 minutes until the top is golden brown.

VARIATION
For a less strongly flavoured dish, alternate the layers of celeriac with potato. Slice the potato, cook until almost tender, then drain well before assembling the dish.

TOMATO AND BASIL TART

IN FRANCE, PATISSERIES DISPLAY MOUTH-WATERING SAVOURY TARTS IN THEIR WINDOWS. THIS IS A VERY SIMPLE YET EXTREMELY TASTY TART MADE WITH RICH SHORTCRUST PASTRY, TOPPED WITH SLICES OF MOZZARELLA CHEESE AND TOMATOES AND ENRICHED WITH OLIVE OIL AND BASIL LEAVES.

SERVES FOUR

INGREDIENTS
   150g/5oz mozzarella,
      thinly sliced
   4 large tomatoes, thickly sliced
   about 10 basil leaves
   30ml/2 tbsp olive oil
   2 garlic cloves, thinly sliced
   sea salt and freshly ground
      black pepper
For the pastry
   115g/4oz plain flour
   50g/2oz butter or margarine
   1 egg yolk
   pinch of salt

1 To prepare the pastry, mix together the flour and salt, then rub in the butter and egg yolk. Add enough cold water to make a smooth dough and knead lightly on a floured surface. Place in a plastic bag and chill for about 1 hour.

2 Preheat the oven to 190°C/375°F/ Gas 5. Remove the pastry from the fridge and allow about 10 minutes for it to return to room temperature and then roll out into a 20cm/8in round. Press into the base of a 20cm/8in flan dish or tin. Prick all over with a fork and then bake in the oven for about 10 minutes until firm but not brown. Allow to cool slightly. Reduce the oven temperature to 180°C/350°F/ Gas 4.

3 Arrange the mozzarella slices over the pastry base. On top, arrange a single layer of the sliced tomatoes, overlapping them slightly. Dip the basil leaves in olive oil and arrange them on the tomatoes.

4 Scatter the garlic on top, drizzle with the remaining olive oil and season with a little salt and a good sprinkling of black pepper. Bake for 40–45 minutes, until the tomatoes are well cooked. Serve hot.

VEGETABLES JULIENNE <u>WITH A</u> RED PEPPER COULIS

JUST THE RIGHT COURSE FOR THOSE WATCHING THEIR WEIGHT. CHOOSE A SELECTION OF AS MANY VEGETABLES AS YOU FEEL YOU CAN EAT.

<u>SERVES TWO</u>

INGREDIENTS

A selection of vegetables (choose from: carrots, turnips, asparagus, parsnips, courgettes, green beans, broccoli, salsify, cauliflower, mangetouts)

For the red pepper coulis

1 small onion, chopped
1 garlic clove, crushed
15ml/1 tbsp sunflower oil
15ml/1 tbsp water
3 red peppers, roasted and skinned
120ml/8 tbsp fromage frais
squeeze of fresh lemon juice
salt and ground black pepper
sprigs of fresh rosemary and thyme
2 bay leaves
fresh green herbs, to garnish

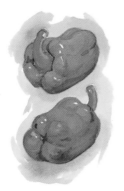

1 Prepare the vegetables by cutting them into thin fingers or small, bite size pieces.

2 Make the coulis. Lightly sauté the onion and garlic in the oil and water for 3 minutes then add the peppers and cook for a further 2 minutes.

3 Pass the coulis through a food processor, then work in the fromage frais, lemon juice and seasoning.

4 Boil some salted water with the fresh rosemary, thyme and bay leaves, and fit a steamer over the top.

5 Arrange the prepared vegetables on the steamer, placing the harder root vegetables at the bottom and steaming these for about 3 minutes.

6 Add the other vegetables according to their natural tenderness and cook for a further 2–4 minutes.

7 Serve the vegetables on plates with the sauce to one side. Garnish with fresh green herbs, if you wish.

VARIATION
The red pepper coulis makes a wonderful sauce for many other dishes. Try it spooned over fresh pasta with lightly steamed or fried courgettes, or use it as a pouring sauce for savoury filled crêpes.

BROCCOLI RISOTTO TORTE

LIKE A SPANISH OMELETTE, THIS IS A SAVOURY CAKE SERVED IN WEDGES. IT IS GOOD COLD OR HOT, AND NEEDS ONLY A SALAD AS AN ACCOMPANIMENT.

SERVES SIX

INGREDIENTS

225g/8oz broccoli, cut into very small florets
1 onion, chopped
2 garlic cloves, crushed
1 large yellow pepper, sliced
30ml/2 tbsp olive oil
50g/2oz/4 tbsp butter
225g/8oz/1¼ cups risotto rice
120ml/4 floz/½ cup dry white wine
1 litre/1¾ pints/4½ cups stock
salt and ground black pepper
115g/4oz fresh or Parmesan cheese, coarsely grated
4 eggs, separated
oil, for greasing
sliced tomato and chopped parsley, to garnish

1 Blanch the broccoli for 3 minutes then drain and reserve.

2 In a large saucepan, gently fry the onion, garlic and pepper in the oil and butter for 5 minutes until they are soft.

3 Stir in the rice, cook for a minute then pour in the wine. Cook, stirring the mixture until the liquid is absorbed.

4 Pour in the stock, season well, bring to the boil then lower to a simmer. Cook for 20 minutes, stirring occasionally.

5 Meanwhile, grease a 25cm/10in round deep cake tin and line the base with a disc of greaseproof paper. Preheat the oven to 180°C/350°F/Gas 4.

6 Stir the cheese into the rice, allow the mixture to cool for 5 minutes, then beat in the egg yolks.

7 Whisk the egg whites until they form soft peaks and carefully fold into the rice. Turn into the prepared tin and bake for about 1 hour until risen, golden brown and slightly wobbly in the centre.

8 Allow the torte to cool in the tin, then chill if serving cold. Run a knife round the edge of the tin and shake out onto a serving plate. If liked, garnish with sliced tomato and chopped parsley.

VEGETABLE AND HERB KEBABS WITH GREEN PEPPERCORN SAUCE

OTHER VEGETABLES CAN BE INCLUDED IN THESE KEBABS, DEPENDING ON WHAT IS AVAILABLE AT THE TIME. THE GREEN PEPPERCORN SAUCE IS ALSO AN EXCELLENT ACCOMPANIMENT TO MANY OTHER DISHES.

SERVES FOUR

INGREDIENTS
8 bamboo skewers soaked in water for
  1 hour
24 mushrooms
16 cherry tomatoes
16 large basil leaves
16 thick slices of courgette
16 large mint leaves
16 squares of red sweet pepper
To baste
120ml/4floz/½ cup melted butter
1 clove garlic, peeled and crushed
15ml/1 tbsp crushed green peppercorns
salt
For the green peppercorn sauce
50g/2oz/¼ cup butter
45ml/3 tbsp brandy
250ml/8fl oz/1 cup double cream
5ml/1 tsp crushed green peppercorns

1 Thread the vegetables on to bamboo skewers. Place the basil leaves immediately next to the tomatoes, and the mint leaves wrapped around the courgette slices.

2 Mix the basting ingredients and baste the kebabs thoroughly. Place the skewers on a barbecue or under the grill, turning and basting regularly until the vegetables are just cooked – about 5–7 minutes.

3 Heat the butter for the sauce in a frying pan, then add the brandy and light it. When the flames have died down, stir in the cream and the peppercorns. Cook for approximately 2 minutes, stirring all the time. Serve the kebabs with the green peppercorn sauce.

FESTIVE LENTIL AND NUT ROAST

SERVE WITH VEGETARIAN GRAVY,
CRANBERRIES AND FRENCH
PARSLEY.

SERVES SIX TO EIGHT

INGREDIENTS
    115g/4oz/⅔ cup red lentils
    115g/4oz/1 cup hazelnuts
    115g/4oz/1 cup walnuts
    1 large carrot
    2 celery sticks
    1 large onion, sliced
    115g/4oz mushrooms
    50g/2oz/4 tbsp butter
    10ml/2 tsp mild curry powder
    30ml/2 tbsp tomato ketchup
    30ml/2 tbsp soy sauce
    1 egg, beaten
    10ml/2 tsp salt
    60ml/4 tbsp fresh parsley, chopped
    150ml/¼ pint/⅔ cup water

1 Soak the lentils for 1 hour in cold water then drain well. Grind the nuts in a food processor until quite fine but not too smooth. Set the nuts aside.

2 Chop the carrot, celery, onion and mushrooms into small chunks, then pass them through a food processor or blender until they are quite finely chopped.

3 Fry the vegetables gently in the butter for 5 minutes then stir in the curry powder and cook for a minute. Cool.

4 Mix the lentils with the nuts, vegetables and remaining ingredients.

5 Grease and line the base and sides of a long 1 kg/2 lb loaf tin with greaseproof paper or a sheet of foil. Press the mixture into the tin. Preheat the oven to 190°C/375°F/Gas 5.

6 Bake for about 1–1¼ hours until just firm, covering the top with a butter paper or piece of foil if it starts to burn. Allow the mixture to stand for about 15 minutes before you turn it out and peel off the paper. It will be fairly soft when cut as it is a moist loaf.

VEGETARIAN GRAVY

MAKE UP A LARGE BATCH AND
FREEZE IT IN SMALL CONTAINERS
READY TO REHEAT AND SERVE.

MAKES ABOUT 1 LITRE/1¾ PINTS

INGREDIENTS
    1 large red onion, sliced
    3 turnips, sliced
    3 celery sticks, sliced
    115g/4oz open cut mushrooms, halved
    2 whole garlic cloves
    90ml/6 tbsp sunflower oil
    1.5 litres/2½ pints/6 cups vegetable
       stock or water
    45ml/3 tbsp soy sauce
    good pinch of granulated sugar
    salt and ground black pepper

1 Cook the vegetables and garlic on a moderately high heat with the oil in a large saucepan, stirring occasionally until nicely browned but not singed. This should take about 15-20 minutes.

2 Add the stock or water and soy sauce, bring to the boil then cover and simmer for another 20 minutes.

3 Purée the vegetables, adding a little of the stock, and return them to the pan by rubbing the pulp through a sieve with the back of a ladle or wooden spoon.

4 Taste for seasoning and add the sugar. Freeze at least half of the gravy to use later and reheat the rest to serve with the rice and peas or lentil and nut roast.

GREEK STUFFED VEGETABLES

VEGETABLES SUCH AS PEPPERS MAKE WONDERFUL CONTAINERS FOR SAVOURY FILLINGS. THICK, CREAMY GREEK YOGURT IS THE IDEAL ACCOMPANIMENT.

SERVES THREE TO SIX

INGREDIENTS

1 medium aubergine
1 large green pepper
2 large tomatoes
1 large onion, chopped
2 garlic cloves, crushed
45ml/3 tbsp olive oil
200g/7oz/1 cup brown rice
600ml/1 pint/2½ cups stock
75g/3oz/¾ cup pine nuts
50g/2oz/⅓ cup currants
salt and ground black pepper
45ml/3 tbsp fresh dill, chopped
45ml/3 tbsp fresh parsley, chopped
15ml/1 tbsp fresh mint, chopped
extra olive oil, to sprinkle
natural Greek yogurt, to serve
fresh sprigs of dill

1 Halve the aubergine, scoop out the flesh with a sharp knife and chop finely. Salt the insides and leave to drain upside down for 20 minutes while you prepare the other ingredients.

2 Halve the pepper, seed and core. Cut the tops from the tomatoes, scoop out the insides and chop roughly along with the tomato tops.

3 Fry the onion, garlic and chopped aubergine in the oil for 10 minutes, then stir in the rice and cook for 2 minutes.

4 Add the tomato flesh, stock, pine nuts, currants and seasoning. Bring to the boil, cover and simmer for 15 minutes then stir in the fresh herbs.

5 Blanch the aubergines and green pepper halves in boiling water for about 3 minutes, then drain them upside down.

6 Spoon the rice filling into all six vegetable 'containers' and place on a lightly greased ovenproof shallow dish.

7 Heat the oven to 190°C/375°F/Gas 5, drizzle over some olive oil and bake the vegetables for 25–30 minutes. Serve hot, topped with spoonfuls of natural yogurt and dill sprigs.

THAI NOODLES <u>WITH</u> CHINESE CHIVES

THIS RECIPE REQUIRES A LITTLE TIME FOR PREPARATION, BUT THE COOKING TIME IS VERY FAST.
EVERYTHING IS COOKED SPEEDILY IN A HOT WOK AND SHOULD BE EATEN AT ONCE.

SERVES FOUR

INGREDIENTS

350g/12oz dried rice noodles
1cm/½ in fresh root ginger, grated
30ml/2 tbsp light soy sauce
45ml/3 tbsp vegetable oil
225g/8oz Quorn, cut into small cubes
2 garlic cloves, crushed
1 large onion, cut into thin wedges
115g/4oz fried bean curd, thinly sliced
1 green chilli, seeded
 and finely sliced
175g/6oz beansprouts
115g/4oz Chinese chives, cut into
 5cm/2in lengths
50g/2oz roasted peanuts, ground
30ml/ 2tbsp dark soy sauce
30ml/2 tbsp chopped fresh coriander
1 lemon, cut into wedges

1 Place the noodles in a large bowl, cover with warm water and soak for 20–30 minutes, then drain. Blend together the ginger, light soy sauce and 15ml/1 tbsp of the oil in a bowl. Stir in the Quorn and set aside for 10 minutes. Drain, reserving the marinade.

2 Heat 15ml/1 tbsp of the oil in a frying pan and fry the garlic for a few seconds. Add the Quorn and stir-fry for 3–4 minutes. Then transfer to a plate and set aside.

3 Heat the remaining oil in the wok or frying pan and stir-fry the onion for 3–4 minutes until softened and tinged with brown. Add the bean curd and chilli, stir-fry briefly and then add the noodles. Stir-fry for 4–5 minutes.

4 Stir in the beansprouts, Chinese chives and most of the ground peanuts, reserving a little for the garnish. Stir well, then add the Quorn, the dark soy sauce and the reserved marinade.

5 When hot, spoon on to serving plates and garnish with the remaining ground peanuts, coriander and lemon wedges.

COOK'S TIP
Quorn makes this a vegetarian meal, however thinly sliced pork or chicken could be used instead. Stir-fry it initially for 4–5 minutes.

SHEPHERDESS PIE

*A NO-MEAT VERSION OF THE
TIMELESS CLASSIC, THIS DISH
CONTAINS NO DAIRY PRODUCTS,
SO IS SUITABLE FOR VEGANS.*

SERVES SIX TO EIGHT

INGREDIENTS

1kg/2lb potatoes
45ml/3 tbsp extra virgin olive oil
salt and ground black pepper
1 large onion, chopped
1 green pepper, chopped
2 carrots, coarsely grated
2 garlic cloves
45ml/3 tbsp sunflower oil or margarine
115g/4oz mushrooms, chopped
2 × 400g/14oz cans aduki beans
600ml/1 pint/2½ cups stock
5ml/1 tsp vegetable yeast extract
2 bay leaves
5ml/1 tsp dried mixed herbs
dried breadcrumbs or chopped nuts,
  to sprinkle

1 Boil the potatoes in the skins until tender, then drain, reserving a little of the water to moisten them.

2 Mash well, mixing in the olive oil and seasoning until you have a smooth purée. (Potatoes are easier to peel when boiled in their skins. This also preserves vitamins.)

3 Gently fry the onion, pepper, carrots and garlic in the sunflower oil or margarine for about 5 minutes until they are soft. Preheat the grill.

4 Stir in the mushrooms and drained beans and cook for a further 2 minutes, then add the stock, yeast extract, bay leaves and mixed herbs. Simmer for 15 minutes.

5 Remove the bay leaves and empty the vegetables into a shallow ovenproof dish. Spoon on the potatoes in dollops and sprinkle over the crumbs or nuts. Grill until golden brown.

ROAST ASPARAGUS CRÊPES

ROAST ASPARAGUS IS DELICIOUS AND GOOD ENOUGH TO EAT JUST AS IT COMES. HOWEVER, FOR A REALLY SPLENDID STARTER, TRY THIS SIMPLE RECIPE. EITHER MAKE SIX LARGE OR TWICE AS MANY COCKTAIL-SIZE PANCAKES TO USE WITH SMALLER STEMS OF ASPARAGUS.

SERVES SIX

INGREDIENTS
   90–120ml/6–8 tbsp olive oil
   450g/1lb fresh asparagus
   175g/6oz mascarpone cheese
   60ml/4 tbsp single cream
   25g/1oz Parmesan cheese, grated
   sea salt
For the pancakes
   175g/6oz plain flour
   2 eggs
   350ml/12fl oz/1½ cups milk
   vegetable oil, for frying
   pinch of salt

1 To make the pancake batter, mix the flour with the salt in a large bowl, food processor or blender, then add the eggs and milk and beat or process to make a smooth, fairly thin batter.

2 Heat a little oil in a large frying pan and add a small amount of batter, swirling the pan to coat the base evenly. Cook over a moderate heat for about 1 minute, then flip over and cook the other side until golden. Set aside and cook the rest of the pancakes in the same way; the mixture makes about six large or 12 smaller pancakes.

3 Preheat the oven to 180°C/350°F/ Gas 4 and lightly grease a large shallow ovenproof dish or roasting tin with some of the olive oil.

4 Trim the asparagus by placing on a board and cutting off the bases. Using a small sharp knife, peel away the woody ends, if necessary.

5 Arrange the asparagus in a single layer in the dish, trickle over the remaining olive oil, rolling the asparagus to coat each one thoroughly. Sprinkle with a little salt and then roast in the oven for about 8–12 minutes until tender (the cooking time depends on the stem thickness).

6 Blend the mascarpone cheese with the cream and Parmesan cheese and spread a generous tablespoonful over each of the pancakes, leaving a little extra for the topping. Preheat the grill.

7 Divide the asparagus spears among the pancakes, roll up and arrange in a single layer in an ovenproof dish. Spoon over the remaining cheese mixture and then place under a moderate grill for 4–5 minutes, until heated through and golden brown. Serve at once.

SALADS &
SIDE DISHES

~

HASSELBACK POTATOES

A VERY UNUSUAL WAY WITH POTATOES. EACH POTATO HALF IS SLICED ALMOST TO THE BASE AND THEN ROASTED WITH OIL AND BUTTER. THE CRISPY POTATOES ARE THEN COATED IN AN ORANGE GLAZE AND RETURNED TO THE OVEN UNTIL DEEP GOLDEN BROWN AND CRUNCHY.

SERVES FOUR TO SIX

INGREDIENTS
    4 large potatoes
    25g/1oz butter, melted
    45ml/3 tbsp olive oil
For the glaze
    juice of 1 orange
    grated rind of ½ orange
    15ml/1 tbsp demerara sugar
    freshly ground black pepper

1 Preheat the oven to 190°C/375°F/ Gas 5. Cut each potato in half lengthways, place flat-side down and then cut down as if making very thin slices, but leaving the bottom 1cm/½in intact.

2 Place the potatoes in a large roasting dish. Using a pastry brush, coat the potatoes generously with the melted butter and pour the olive oil over the base and around the potatoes.

3 Bake the potatoes in the oven for 40–50 minutes until they begin to brown. Baste occasionally during cooking.

4 Meanwhile, place the orange juice, orange rind and sugar in a small saucepan and heat gently, stirring until the sugar has dissolved. Simmer for 3–4 minutes until the glaze is fairly thick and then remove from the heat.

5 When the potatoes begin to brown, brush all over with the orange glaze and return to the oven to roast for a further 15 minutes or until the potatoes are a deep golden brown. Serve at once.

TURNIP TOPS WITH PARMESAN AND GARLIC

TURNIP TOPS HAVE A PRONOUNCED FLAVOUR AND ARE GOOD WHEN COOKED WITH OTHER STRONG-FLAVOURED INGREDIENTS SUCH AS ONIONS, GARLIC AND PARMESAN CHEESE. THEY DO NOT NEED LONG COOKING AS THE LEAVES ARE QUITE TENDER.

SERVES FOUR

INGREDIENTS

45ml/3 tbsp olive oil
2 garlic cloves, crushed
4 spring onions, sliced
350g/12oz turnip tops, thinly sliced,
   tough stalk removed
50g/2oz Parmesan cheese, grated
salt and freshly ground black pepper
shavings of Parmesan cheese,
   to garnish

1 Heat the olive oil in a large saucepan and fry the garlic for a few seconds. Add the spring onions, stir-fry for 2 minutes and then add the turnip tops.

2 Stir-fry for a few minutes so that the greens are coated in oil, then add about 50ml/2fl oz/¼ cup water. Bring to the boil, cover and simmer until the greens are tender. Stir occasionally and do not allow the pan to boil dry.

3 Bring the liquid to the boil and allow the excess to evaporate and then stir in the Parmesan cheese. Serve at once with extra shavings of cheese, if liked.

PEAS WITH BABY ONIONS AND CREAM

IDEALLY, USE FRESH PEAS AND FRESH BABY ONIONS. FROZEN PEAS ARE AN ACCEPTABLE SUBSTITUTE IF FRESH ONES AREN'T AVAILABLE, BUT FROZEN ONIONS TEND TO BE INSIPID AND ARE NOT WORTH USING. ALTERNATIVELY, USE THE WHITE PARTS OF SPRING ONIONS.

SERVES FOUR

INGREDIENTS
175g/6oz baby onions
15g/½ oz butter
900g/2lb fresh peas (about
    350g/12oz shelled or frozen)
150ml/¼ pint/⅔ cup double cream
15g/½oz plain flour
10ml/2 tsp chopped fresh parsley
15–30ml/1–2 tbsp lemon juice
    (optional)
salt and freshly ground black pepper

1 Peel the onions and halve them if necessary. Melt the butter in a flame-proof casserole and fry the onions for 5–6 minutes over a moderate heat, until they begin to be flecked with brown.

3 Using a small whisk, blend the cream with the flour. Remove the pan from the heat and stir in the combined cream and flour, parsley and seasoning to taste.

4 Cook over a gentle heat for about 3–4 minutes, until the sauce is thick. Taste and adjust the seasoning; add a little lemon juice to sharpen, if liked.

2 Add the peas and stir-fry for a few minutes. Add 120ml/4fl oz/¼ cup water and bring to the boil. Partially cover and simmer for about 10 minutes until both the peas and onions are tender. There should be a thin layer of water on the base of the pan – add a little more water if necessary or, if there is too much liquid, remove the lid and increase the heat until the liquid is reduced.

RUNNER BEANS WITH GARLIC

DELICATE AND FRESH-TASTING FLAGEOLET BEANS AND GARLIC ADD A DISTINCT FRENCH FLAVOUR TO THIS SIMPLE SIDE DISH. SERVE TO ACCOMPANY ROAST LAMB OR VEAL.

SERVES FOUR

INGREDIENTS
225g/8oz flageolet beans
15ml/1 tbsp olive oil
25g/1oz butter
1 onion, finely chopped
1–2 garlic cloves, crushed
3–4 tomatoes, peeled and chopped
350g/12oz runner beans, prepared
  and sliced
150ml/¼ pint/⅔ cup white wine
150ml/¼ pint/⅔ cup vegetable stock
30ml/2 tbsp chopped fresh parsley
salt and freshly ground black pepper

1 Place the flageolet beans in a large saucepan of water, bring to the boil and simmer for ¾–1 hour until tender. Drain.

2 Heat the oil and butter in a large frying pan and sauté the onion and garlic for 3–4 minutes until soft. Add the chopped tomatoes and continue cooking over a gentle heat until they are soft.

3 Stir the flageolet beans into the onion and tomato mixture, then add the runner beans, wine, stock, and a little salt. Stir well. Cover and simmer for 5–10 minutes until the runner beans are tender.

4 Increase the heat to reduce the liquid, then stir in the parsley and season with a little more salt, if necessary, and pepper.

SHIITAKE FRIED RICE

SHIITAKE MUSHROOMS HAVE A STRONG MEATY MUSHROOMY AROMA AND FLAVOUR. THIS IS A VERY EASY RECIPE TO MAKE, AND ALTHOUGH IT IS A SIDE DISH IT CAN ALMOST BE A MEAL IN ITSELF.

SERVES FOUR

INGREDIENTS
2 eggs
45ml/3 tbsp vegetable oil
350g/12oz shiitake mushrooms
8 spring onions, sliced diagonally
1 garlic clove, crushed
½ green pepper, chopped
25g/1oz butter
175–225g/6–8oz long grain rice, cooked
15ml/1 tbsp medium dry sherry
30ml/2 tbsp dark soy sauce
15ml/1 tbsp chopped fresh coriander
salt

1 Beat the eggs with 15ml/1 tbsp cold water and season with a little salt.

2 Heat 15ml/1 tbsp of the oil in a wok or large frying pan, pour in the eggs and cook to make a large omelette. Lift the sides of the omelette and tilt the wok so that the uncooked egg can run underneath and be cooked. Roll up the omelette and slice thinly.

3 Remove and discard the mushroom stalks if tough and slice the caps thinly, halving them if they are large.

4 Heat 15ml/1 tbsp of the remaining oil in the wok and stir-fry the spring onions and garlic for 3–4 minutes until softened but not brown. Transfer them to a plate using a slotted spoon.

5 Add the pepper, stir-fry for about 2–3 minutes, then add the butter and the remaining 15ml/1 tbsp of oil. As the butter begins to sizzle, add the mushrooms and stir-fry over a moderate heat for 3–4 minutes until soft.

6 Loosen the rice grains as much as possible. Pour the sherry over the mushrooms and then stir in the rice.

7 Heat the rice over a moderate heat, stirring all the time to prevent it sticking. If the rice seems very dry, add a little more oil. Stir in the reserved onions and omelette slices, the soy sauce and coriander. Cook for a few minutes until heated through and serve.

COOK'S TIP
Unlike risotto, for which rice is cooked along with the other ingredients, Chinese fried rice is always made using cooked rice. If you use 175–225g/6–8oz uncooked long grain, you will get about 450–500g/16–20oz cooked rice, enough for four people.

GLAZED CARROTS WITH CIDER

THIS RECIPE IS EXTREMELY SIMPLE TO MAKE. THE CARROTS ARE COOKED IN THE MINIMUM OF LIQUID TO BRING OUT THE BEST OF THEIR FLAVOUR, AND THE CIDER ADDS A PLEASANT SHARPNESS.

SERVES FOUR

INGREDIENTS
  450g/1lb young carrots
  25g/1oz butter
  15ml/1 tbsp brown sugar
  120ml/4fl oz/½ cup cider
  60ml/4 tbsp vegetable stock or water
  5ml/1 tsp Dijon mustard
  15ml/1 tbsp finely chopped fresh
    parsley

1 Trim the tops and bottoms of the carrots. Peel or scrape them. Using a sharp knife, cut them into julienne strips.

2 Melt the butter in a frying pan, add the carrots and sauté for 4–5 minutes, stirring frequently. Sprinkle over the sugar and cook, stirring for 1 minute or until the sugar has dissolved.

3 Add the cider and stock or water, bring to the boil and stir in the Dijon mustard. Partially cover the pan and simmer for about 10–12 minutes until the carrots are just tender. Remove the lid and continue cooking until the liquid has reduced to a thick sauce.

4 Remove the saucepan from the heat, stir in the parsley and then spoon into a warmed serving dish. Serve as an accompaniment to grilled meat or fish or with a vegetarian dish.

COOK'S TIP
If the carrots are cooked before the liquid in the saucepan has reduced, transfer the carrots to a serving dish and rapidly boil the liquid until thick. Pour over the carrots and sprinkle with parsley.

CARROT, APPLE AND ORANGE COLESLAW

THIS DISH IS AS DELICIOUS AS IT IS EASY TO MAKE. THE GARLIC AND HERB DRESSING ADDS THE NECESSARY CONTRAST TO THE SWEETNESS OF THE SALAD.

SERVES FOUR

INGREDIENTS
  350g/12oz young carrots,
    finely grated
  2 eating apples
  15ml/1 tbsp lemon juice
  1 large orange
For the dressing
  45ml/3 tbsp olive oil
  60ml/4 tbsp sunflower oil
  45ml/3 tbsp lemon juice
  1 garlic clove, crushed
  60ml/4 tbsp natural yogurt
  15ml/1 tbsp chopped mixed fresh
    herbs: tarragon, parsley, chives
  salt and freshly ground black pepper

1 Place the carrots in a large serving bowl. Quarter the apples, remove the core and then slice thinly. Sprinkle with the lemon juice to prevent them dis-colouring and then add to the carrots.

2 Using a sharp knife, remove the peel and pith from the orange and then separate into segments.

3 To make the dressing, place all the ingredients in a jar with a tight-fitting lid and shake vigorously to blend.

4 Just before serving, pour the dressing over the salad and toss well together.

CRUNCHY CABBAGE SALAD WITH PESTO MAYONNAISE

Both the pesto and the mayonnaise can be made for this dish. However, if time is short, you can buy them both ready-prepared and it will taste just as good. Add the dressing just before serving to prevent the cabbage going soggy.

SERVES FOUR TO SIX

INGREDIENTS
    1 small or ½ medium white cabbage
    3–4 carrots, grated
    4 spring onions, finely sliced
    25–40g/1–1½oz pine nuts
    15ml/1 tbsp chopped fresh mixed
        herbs; parsley, basil and chervil
For the pesto mayonnaise
    1 egg yolk
    about 10ml/2 tsp lemon juice
    200ml/7fl oz/⅞ cup sunflower oil
    10ml/2 tsp pesto
    60ml/4 tbsp natural yogurt
    salt and freshly ground black pepper

1 To make the mayonnaise, place the egg yolk in a blender or food processor and process with the lemon juice. With the machine running, very slowly add the oil, pouring it more quickly as the mayonnaise emulsifies. Season to taste with salt and pepper and a little more lemon juice if necessary. Alternatively, make by hand using a balloon whisk.

2 Spoon 75ml/5 tbsp of mayonnaise into a bowl and stir in the pesto and yogurt, beating well to make a fairly thin dressing. (The remaining mayonnaise will keep for about 3–4 weeks in a screw-top jar in the fridge.)

3 Using a food processor or a sharp knife, thinly slice the cabbage and place in a large salad bowl.

4 Add the carrots and spring onions, together with the pine nuts and herbs, mixing thoroughly with your hands. Stir the pesto dressing into the salad or serve separately in a small dish if preferred.

PEPERONATA WITH RAISINS

*SLICED ROASTED PEPPERS IN
DRESSING WITH VINEGAR-SOAKED
RAISINS MAKE A TASTY SIDE
SALAD WHICH COMPLEMENTS
MANY OTHER DISHES.*

SERVES TWO TO FOUR

INGREDIENTS

90ml/6 tbsp sliced peppers in olive oil,
   drained
15ml/1 tbsp onion, chopped
30ml/2 tbsp balsamic vinegar
45ml/3 tbsp raisins
30ml/2 tbsp fresh parsley, chopped
ground black pepper

1 Toss the peppers with the onion and
leave to steep for an hour.

2 Put the vinegar and raisins in a small
saucepan and heat for a minute, then
allow to cool.

3 Mix all the ingredients together
thoroughly and spoon into a serving bowl.
Serve lightly chilled.

COOK'S TIP
Peperonata is one of the classic Italian
antipasto dishes, served at the start of
each meal with crusty bread to mop up
the delicious juices. Try serving shavings
of fresh Parmesan cheese alongside, or
buy a good selection of green and black
olives to accompany the peperonata.
Small baby tomatoes will complete the
antipasto.

FRENCH BEAN SALAD

ALTHOUGH BEAN SALADS ARE DELICIOUS SERVED WITH A SIMPLE VINAIGRETTE DRESSING, THIS DISH IS A LITTLE MORE ELABORATE. IT DOES, HOWEVER, ENHANCE THE FRESH FLAVOUR OF THE BEANS.

SERVES FOUR

INGREDIENTS
    450g/1lb French beans
    15ml/1 tbsp olive oil
    25g/1oz butter
    ½ garlic clove, crushed
    50g/2oz fresh white breadcrumbs
    15ml/1 tbsp chopped fresh
       parsley
    1 egg, hard-boiled and finely chopped
For the dressing
    30ml/2 tbsp olive oil
    30ml/2 tbsp sunflower oil
    10ml/2 tsp white wine vinegar
    ½ garlic clove, crushed
    1.5ml/¼ tsp French mustard
    pinch of sugar
    pinch of salt

1 Trim the French beans and cook in boiling salted water for 5–6 minutes until tender. Drain the beans and refresh them under cold running water and place in a serving bowl.

2 Make the salad dressing by blending the oils, vinegar, garlic, mustard, sugar and salt thoroughly together. Pour over the beans and toss to mix.

COOK'S TIP
For a more substantial salad, boil about 450g/1lb scrubbed new potatoes until tender, cool and then cut them into bite-size chunks. Stir into the French beans and then add the dressing.

3 Heat the oil and butter in a frying pan and fry the garlic for 1 minute. Stir in the breadcrumbs and fry over a moderate heat for about 3–4 minutes until golden brown, stirring frequently.

4 Remove the pan from the heat and stir in the parsley and then the egg. Sprinkle the breadcrumb mixture over the French beans. Serve warm or at room temperature.

R A D I S H , M A N G O AND A P P L E S A L A D

RADISH IS A YEAR-ROUND VEGETABLE AND THIS SALAD CAN BE SERVED AT ANY TIME OF YEAR, WITH ITS CLEAN, CRISP TASTES AND MELLOW FLAVOURS. SERVE WITH SMOKED FISH, SUCH AS ROLLS OF SMOKED SALMON, OR WITH CONTINENTAL HAM OR SALAMI.

SERVES FOUR

INGREDIENTS
  10–15 radishes
  1 dessert apple, peeled cored and
    thinly sliced
  2 celery stalks, thinly sliced
  1 small ripe mango, peeled and cut
    into small chunks
For the dressing
  120ml/4fl oz/½ cup soured cream
  10ml/2 tsp creamed horseradish
  15ml/1 tbsp chopped fresh dill
  salt and freshly ground black pepper
  sprigs of dill, to garnish

3 Cut through the mango lengthways either side of the stone. Make even criss-cross cuts through each side section. Take each one and bend it back to separate the cubes. Remove the mango cubes with a small knife and add to the bowl. Pour the dressing over the vegetables and fruit and stir gently so that all the ingredients are coated in the dressing. When ready to serve, spoon the salad into an attractive salad bowl and garnish with sprigs of dill.

1 To prepare the dressing, blend together the soured cream, horseradish and dill in a small jug or bowl and season with a little salt and pepper.

2 Top and tail the radishes and then slice them thinly. Add to a bowl together with the thinly sliced apple and celery.

POTATO SALAD <u>WITH</u> CURRY PLANT MAYONNAISE

POTATO SALAD CAN BE MADE WELL IN ADVANCE AND IS THEREFORE A USEFUL BUFFET DISH. ITS POPULARITY MEANS THAT THERE ARE VERY RARELY ANY LEFTOVERS.

SERVES SIX

INGREDIENTS
  salt
  1kg/2lb new potatoes, in skins
  300ml/½ pint/1¼ cups shop-bought
    mayonnaise
  6 curry plant leaves, roughly chopped
  black pepper
  mixed lettuce or other salad greens, to
    serve

1 Place the potatoes in a pan of salted water and boil for 15 minutes or until tender. Drain and place in a large bowl to cool slightly.

2 Mix the mayonnaise with the curry plant leaves and black pepper. Stir these into the potatoes while they are still warm. Leave to cool, then serve on a bed of mixed lettuce or other assorted salad leaves.

GARDEN SALAD AND GARLIC CROSTINI

DRESS A COLOURFUL MIXTURE OF SALAD LEAVES WITH GOOD OLIVE OIL AND FRESH LEMON JUICE.

SERVES FOUR TO SIX

INGREDIENTS
   3 thick slices day-old bread
   120ml/4fl oz/½ cup extra virgin olive oil
   garlic clove, cut
   ½ small cos or romaine lettuce
   ½ small oak leaf lettuce
   25g/1oz rocket leaves or cress
   25g/1oz fresh flat leaf parsley
   a few leaves and flowers of nasturtium
   flowers of pansy and pot marigold
   a handful of young dandelion leaves
   sea salt flakes and ground black pepper
   juice of 1 fresh lemon

1 Cut the bread into medium size dice about 1cm/½in square.

2 Heat half the oil gently in a frying pan and fry the bread cubes in it, tossing them until they are well coated and lightly browned. Remove and cool.

3 Rub the inside of a large salad bowl with the garlic and discard. Pour the rest of the oil into the bottom of the bowl.

4 Wash, dry and tear the leaves into bite size pieces and pile them into the bowl. Season with salt and pepper. Cover and keep chilled until ready to serve.

5 To serve, toss the leaves in the oil at the bottom of the bowl, then sprinkle with the lemon juice and toss again. Scatter over the crostini and serve immediately.

INDEX

aduki beans: burgers, 30
  shepherdess pie, 80
artichokes with garlic and herb
    butter, 22
asparagus: asparagus soup, 12
  roast asparagus crêpes, 81
aubergines: loofah and aubergine
    ratatouille, 50
avocados: guacamole, 18
  warm avocados with tangy
    topping, 26

balti-style cauliflower with
    tomatoes, 31
borlotti beans: ricotta and borlotti
    bean pâté, 20
broccoli: broccoli risotto torte, 74
  hot broccoli tartlets, 38
bruschetta with goats' cheese and
    tapenade, 26
Brussels sprouts: festive jalousie,
    68
burgers, aduki bean, 30

cabbage salad with pesto
    mayonnaise, 90
cannellini beans, spinach
    and, 59
carrots: carrot, apple and orange
    coleslaw, 88
  glazed carrots with cider, 88
cassava and vegetable
    kebabs, 61
cauliflower: balti-style, with
    tomatoes, 31
  cauliflower and egg cheese, 39
  cauliflower and mushroom
    gougère, 64
celeriac: celeriac and blue cheese
    roulade, 49
  celeriac gratin, 70
cheese: baked leeks with cheese
    and yogurt topping, 63
  bruschetta with goats' cheese
    and tapenade, 26
  cauliflower and egg cheese, 39
  celeriac and blue cheese
    roulade, 49
  macaroni soufflé, 29
  ricotta and borlotti bean pâté, 20
  rocket and grilled chèvre
    salad, 19
  spinach in filo with three
    cheeses, 65
  sweetcorn and cheese
    pasties, 60
chick-peas: hot sour chick-
    peas, 37
  turnip and chick-pea
    cobbler, 62
coleslaw: carrot, apple and
    orange, 88
courgettes, baked, 40
croûtons, Stilton, 11

dolmades, 25

eddo, carrot and parsnip
    medley, 44
eggs flamenco, 66

French bean salad, 92

garden salad and garlic
    crostini, 95
garlic: garlic mushrooms, 16
  roast garlic with croûtons, 16
gazpacho, 14

gnocchi, marrows with, 47
gougère, cauliflower and
    mushroom, 64
gravy, vegetarian, 76
Greek stuffed vegetables, 78
guacamole, 18

hasselback potatoes, 83

Italian roast peppers, 46

jalousie, festive, 68
Jerusalem artichokes: artichoke
    rösti, 34
  artichoke timbales with spinach
    sauce, 34

kebabs, 61, 75
kitchiri, 41
kohlrabi stuffed with peppers, 56

leeks: baked leeks with cheese
    and yogurt topping, 63
  in egg and lemon sauce, 42
  leek soufflé, 57
lentils: festive lentil and nut
    roast, 76

kitchiri, 41
loofah and aubergine
    ratatouille, 50

macaroni soufflé, 29
marrow: baked marrow in parsley
    sauce, 67
  marrows with gnocchi, 47
Mediterranean vegetables with
    tahini, 24
minestrone, classic, 13

mushrooms: garlic mushrooms, 16
  mushrooms on toast, 20
  shiitake fried rice, 87
  stuffed mushrooms, 36
  tagliatelle fungi, 52
  wild mushrooms in brioche, 54
  wild mushrooms with
    pancakes, 54

noodles: Thai noodles with
    Chinese chives, 79
nuts: festive lentil and nut
    roast, 76

pancakes, 54, 81
parsnip and chestnut
    croquettes, 32
pasties, sweetcorn and cheese, 60
pâté, ricotta and borlotti bean, 20
peanut butter fingers, 43
pear and watercress soup, 11
peas with baby onions, 85
peperonata with raisins, 91
peppers: eggs flamenco, 66
  Italian roast peppers, 46
  kohlrabi stuffed with, 56
  peperonata with raisins, 91

vegetables julienne with a red
    pepper coulis, 72
pies: festive jalousie, 68
pizzas, 33, 51
plantain appetizer, 23
potatoes: hasselback, 83
  peanut butter fingers, 43
  potato salad with curry plant
    mayonnaise, 94
  shepherdess pie, 80

radicchio pizza, 51
radish, mango and apple salad, 93
ravioli, spinach, 58
rice: broccoli risotto torte, 74
  dolmades, 25
  kitchiri, 41
  shiitake fried rice, 87
ricotta and borlotti bean pâté, 20
rocket and grilled chèvre salad, 19
runner beans with garlic, 86

salads, 19, 88–95
shepherdess pie, 80
shiitake fried rice, 87
soufflés, 29, 57
soups, 10–15
spinach: artichoke timbales with
    spinach sauce, 34
  spinach and cannellini
    beans, 59
  spinach in filo with three
    cheeses, 65
  spinach and pepper pizza, 33
  spinach ravioli, 58
Stilton croûtons, 11
sweetcorn and cheese pasties, 60

tagliatelle fungi, 52
tangy fricassée, 53
tapenade, bruschetta with goats'
    cheese and, 26
tarts, 38, 71
Thai noodles with Chinese
    chives, 79
tomatoes: gazpacho, 14
  tomato and basil tart, 71
turnip and chick-pea cobbler, 62
turnip tops with Parmesan and
    garlic, 84

vegetables: classic minestrone, 13
  Greek stuffed vegetables, 78
  Mediterranean vegetables with
    tahini, 24
  tangy fricassée, 53
  vegetable and herb kebabs with
    green peppercorn sauce, 75
  vegetables julienne with a red
    pepper coulis, 72
  winter warmer soup, 15
vine leaves: dolmades, 25

winter warmer soup, 15

yam fritters, 44